Know And Tell The Gospel

Know and Tell
the Gospel

Help for the Reluctant Evangelist

John C Chapman

St Matthias Press
SYDNEY • LONDON

P. 126 '2 Ways to Live', Anglican Information Office, Sydney. Used by permission.

British Library Cataloguing in Publication Data

Chapman, John C.
Know and tell the gospel.
    Help for the reluctant evangelist.
    1. Evangelistic work
    I. Title
    269'.2   BV3790

    ISBN 1 873166 02 8

St Matthias Press, P.O. Box 665, London SW20 8RU

Contents

To Geoffrey Fletcher, evangelist and friend, who over the years has never tired in the work of the gospel. An inspiration and challenge to us all.

Foreword

Evangelism is now higher on the agenda of the Church in this country that it has been for years, both at the national and the local church level.

John Chapman has a proven track record in helping ordinary Christians to clearly and effectively share their faith. In addition to his work in Australian churches he has been a regular visitor to Britain. His lectures have proved enormously popular, and he is as impressive actually doing it as he is talking about evangelism, which is more than can be said about many 'experts'!

Know and Tell the Gospel presents both biblical content of the gospel and practical guidelines to help in sharing it. While the author recognises the need for a simple gospel outline as an aid to clear thinking and concise presentation, there is no dependency on a rigid technique.

We warmly commend this volume, praying that it will prove a timely and effective tool to enable thousands of Christian people to share their faith more confidently and effectively than they have done before.

GAVIN REID
EDDIE GIBBS

Preface

Being engaged in evangelism is exciting, rewarding, the privilege and responsibility of every Christian. I did not always believe so, but have been convinced that this is the perspective of the Bible and therefore of God.

I argue in this book that the unit of evangelism is the individual Christian rather than the Church—that the minister is to be both evangelist and trainer as part of his pastoral/teaching role—that the local church is to train and encourage the individual for an evangelistic task—and that the individual Christian is caught up in this work, which God initiates and controls and for which He provides all the strength needed to accomplish it.

I have been helped greatly over the years by colleagues in the Department of Evangelism, Diocese of Sydney—Geoff Fletcher, Brian Telfer, John Webb, Donald Howard and Luciano Ricci; Phillip Jensen who read the book and offered helpful criticism. I don't hold them responsible for my views but they have been good friends who have listened patiently as ideas were bounced off them, and who have taught me more about evangelism than I have taught them.

Much of the book was delivered at lectures at Great St Helen's in London and the Southampton School of Christian Studies, and I am indebted to the Reverend Dick Lucas and Dr Peter May for the invitations to share in their ministries.

I have always found witnessing difficult and I am thankful for those who over the years have helped me to do the 'work of an evangelist'. My prayer is that we will all realise afresh how kind God has been to us in bringing the gospel to us, and that in gratitude and love we will take the gospel to others.

John Chapman
Department of Evangelism
Sydney, Australia

Part 1

Knowing Why

CHAPTER ONE

What! Another One?

A weary pilgrimage
I remember going to a weekend conference some eighteen months after I was converted, and a girl there asked me if I was a Christian. I answered "Yes."

"Tell me" she said, "what I have to do to become a Christian."

I didn't have the faintest idea where to begin.

As I write this now, I remember well the mixed emotions which swamped me. First, joy—because more than anything else I wanted to see people converted. Second, shame—because I didn't know what to say. Third, anger—(with myself) for allowing such a situation to arise. All these emotions muddled together produced the only possible answer: "I'll take you to someone who can tell you."

So I did that, and she was converted—but not by my words or witness.

That incident left an indelible imprint on my memory, and that day I vowed that such a situation would never happen again. In the future I would know exactly what to say.

So I set out to learn the gospel. Which I did.

Being now thoroughly equipped, I embarked on a flurry of evangelistic activity. The family received the full blast, and a small sermon was delivered at breakfast each day for months! I remember my exasperated father saying one morning, "You don't ever eat your breakfast at church do you? Why must I always have church at breakfast?" It seems a reasonable statement as I look back on it now some thirty years later, although at the time I thought it was a godless rejection of the gospel.

Such feverish activity didn't last long, it was really too hard to sustain, and I noticed that a lot of Christians were not really very concerned about evangelism, it did not seem to worry them. I got the distinct impression that I could be a Christian and not engage in evangelism at all!

Every now and again we were given a 'beat-up' on the Great Commission in Matthew 28:18-20 at church, with the result that my evangelistic activity would begin again. It didn't last long. Evangelism was not a way of life for me.

What helped the go-slow campaign was a new suggestion that the gospel I had learned was really Paul's gospel and not that of Jesus. Jesus' gospel was about the Kingdom of God. Paul's was about the death and resurrection of Jesus. I didn't really know if this constituted a real problem or not. But doubt was now cast on the validity of my gospel so it seemed better to wait until *somebody* sorted it all out.

Then I met Christians who had discovered a 'theological' reason which enabled them not to bother about evangelism. They pointed out that in Ephesians 4:11 one of the gifts which the ascended Christ had given to the Church was that of the evangelists. It was obvious that everybody was not an evangelist. If you were, you did the work. If you weren't, you didn't have to. It was as simple as that. To give them their due they did believe that the evangelists were to be encouraged and helped by us all, but only those who had the gift had to do the work. I decided that as I found evangelism so difficult, then I obviously did not have the gift and so all I had to do was to pray for those who did. From then on whenever I was reminded about the Great Commission to "go into all the world and preach the gospel", I immediately transferred it to the apostles to whom it was originally given and the evangelists whom Christ had provided. It had no direct application to me.

In spite of this I was still uneasy. I felt that I should be trying to lead people to Christ although now I didn't know why. But every time I tried it was so hard that I concluded I did not have the gift.

Someone encouraged me to do evangelism by the suggestion that, although we were not all evangelists, we were all to be 'witnesses' and as such were obliged to take the gospel to the "ends of the earth" (Acts 1:8). It seemed like a good reason until I decided, when I read that verse in its context in the Acts of the Apostles, that the *witnesses* were really those who *had witnessed* Jesus Christ's *resurrection* from the dead. Once again I didn't qualify!

Confusion was now made greater by my own discovery in the Bible that it was God who took the initiative in calling people back to Himself. He predestined them. He drew them back—because He purposed to save them. It was a jolt. I had always thought that my will was totally free and that I had chosen God as mine, not the reverse. This had ramifications in the area of evangelism. I reasoned that, since God had chosen the elect, He would most surely call them to Himself. Doing the work of leading people to Christ seemed less important than I had thought.

Little by little I seemed to find more reasons for doing less.

After I was ordained as a minister I decided that my role was one of a pastor/teacher and not an evangelist. I was to concentrate my efforts and energies on God's people, the Christians. Others would have to do the work of the evangelist. Hand-in-glove with this went the idea that church was meant to build up the Christians and so was an inappropriate place for evangelism.

Thank goodness there were those people who were not deterred by any of this. They plodded on, leading their friends and neighbours to Christ. However when I asked for a biblical reason for this, I was generally given an inadequate or incorrect one.

Why another book?
Some of these problems I resolved sooner than others, and have come to the point where I am convinced that the

Bible clearly states the gospel. I have come to understand that the gospel of the Kingdom of God is not really different from the gospel of the death and resurrection of Jesus for forgiveness of sins. In spite of the specific gift to the Church of the evangelist, and the command of the Great Commission given to the apostles, the Bible teaches that *all* Christians are to directly engage in evangelism.

The Bible also teaches that the individual Christian, not the Church, is the unit for evangelism. To do this work, we all need to be strongly motivated by God's Word. The ordained minister is to be the pastor/teacher of his congregation and as such needs to evangelise, train and encourage the members in this work—as well as doing it himself. The Bible says that even though God does initiate evangelism, and He does call people to Himself, our part in telling the gospel is very real and significant.

I still find evangelism difficult, but I am not discouraged by that. The Bible has shown me that it is a fairly common difficulty, rather than an indication that I do not have some special gift which would make it easier.

Over the last twelve years as I have worked in the Department of Evangelism of the Anglican Church in Sydney, I have encountered such problems many times. I know that there are many people whose experience is parallel to mine and I am writing this book to show how we can arrive at the position where evangelism should become a way of life. It is God's will for *all* His people.

This book is in two sections. In the first, I have set out to show what the Bible says on the questions mentioned earlier. Only a clear biblical perspective on evangelism will enable us to have a proper Christian practice in evangelism.

The second section deals with practical aspects of doing, and of training ourselves and others for evangelism. It has been a surprise and joy to me to see how the most unlikely people have become effective in evangelism through careful training, especially when time was taken to find a method which was suited to the individual's gifts.

The very word 'evangelism' intimidates some people. It

conjures up pictures of emotional meetings where people are manipulated into doing things which in more sober moments they would never dream of doing. Others have had unpleasant experiences of being 'button-holed' by insensitive bores who have talked loudly and at length. The thought of having to become one of them fills most people with dread.

When I use the term 'evangelism' I am talking about the process whereby a person tells other people the gospel of the Lord Jesus Christ with a view to persuading them to put their trust in Jesus as their Lord and Saviour. Whether that telling is a simple chat over coffee or preaching to a hundred thousand makes no difference. Methods vary with people's abilities to use them.

This book is written to help us all find where we, with our gifts and opportunities, fit into the ongoing work of evangelism.

CHAPTER TWO

What is the Gospel?

The gospel and the method

Any book on evangelism must begin with the gospel. An understanding of the gospel governs the way we engage in evangelism. A right understanding of the gospel should lead to right methods; an inadequate understanding will inevitably lead to inadequate practices. A wrong view of the gospel will lead to unhelpful and incorrect ways of doing evangelism.

Where to begin

There are many clear statements of the gospel in the pages of the Bible, but I have chosen the opening verses of the Epistle to the Romans because it is stated so clearly. It answers three basic questions:

1. What is the gospel?
2. What response am I looking for from the gospel?
3. For whom is the gospel intended?

Romans 1:1-5

"Paul, a servant of Christ Jesus, called to be an apostle and set apart for the gospel of God—the gospel he promised beforehand through his prophets in Holy Scriptures regarding his Son, who as to his human nature was a descendant of David, and who through the Spirit (of holiness) was declared with power to be the Son of God by his resurrection from the dead: Jesus Christ our Lord. Through him and for his name's sake, we received grace and apostleship to call people from among all the Gentiles to the obedience that comes from faith."

1. What is the gospel?

Notice in this passage what the apostle tells us about the nature of the gospel.

(a) The gospel is God's

Paul tells us that he is "set apart for the gospel of God" (verse 1). The gospel has its origin in God. He is the first evangelist (Galatians 3:8). The gospel which Jesus preached is described in exactly the same way (Mark 1:14). No man, not even the Lord Jesus, is at liberty to make up his own gospel. The gospel has its origin in God the Father. He is its author and He alone is able to state its content. This fact is both challenging and relieving to any person who preaches the gospel.

Since God has stated the gospel, then care must be taken to make sure I have rightly understood it. That is the challenge. The gospel is a powerful message (Romans 1:16). It is powerful because it comes from God. However, something which is *like* the gospel but isn't the gospel at all, will lack any power to affect in any permanent way the lives of men and women.

The gospel is God's gospel—He is its author and He states its content—and what a relief that is. We don't have to take the responsibility for the reactions of people to it. We didn't make it up! All we have to do is pass on a message. We will have to take full responsibility for the *way we tell* people the gospel but *not the content*. I heard of an undergraduate student who was so outraged by the gospel that he verbally attacked a Christian over the nature of the gospel. The Christian explained to the student that he must take that matter up with a much higher authority since it was not his gospel, but God's gospel. It is a challenge and a relief.

(b) The gospel is not new

"The gospel he promised beforehand through his prophets in the Holy Scriptures" (verse 2). Paul is at pains to show that the gospel he preaches, God's gospel, is not new. Indeed the gospel was promised by God beforehand in the Old Testament prophets. That which is now preached is that which God always had in mind. The way God brings people to Himself has not changed (Isaiah chapter 45; and Galatians 3:8).

The gospel today is in conformity with God's continuing revelation and is the final expression of it. Jesus of Nazareth was recognised as the perfect fulfilment of all that God had foretold in the prophets about His Messiah. The aged Simeon, quoting from Isaiah 42:6 and 49:6, described the child Jesus as "a light for revelation to the Gentiles and for the glory to your people Israel" (Luke 2:29-32).

Peter, in his sermon at the temple in Jerusalem after the healing of the crippled man at the beautiful gate (Acts 3:22), asserts that Jesus is the prophet whom Moses foretold in Deuteronomy 18:15,16.

In his sermon on the day of Pentecost (Acts 2:14-36), Peter claims Jesus as the fulfilment of God's promise in Psalm 132:11 (Acts 2:30), and that it was really Jesus of whom David had spoken in Psalm 16:8-11 (Acts 2:25-28).

(c) The gospel is ALL about Jesus

The gospel "regarding his Son" (verse 3). Here we come to the heart of God's gospel. The gospel is about God's Son. It is a truism to say that the gospel is about Jesus, but it must be said. We are so often side-tracked into thinking that the gospel is about man.

The gospel neither has its origin in man nor does it have its content in man. The gospel is *not* about man and his needs, although these are not unimportant nor are they unrelated. The gospel is all about the Son. It is about Jesus. So when I am evangelising someone I must be speaking about Jesus. If I am not speaking about Jesus, God's unique Son, then I am not preaching God's gospel. When Jesus is preaching God's gospel He is speaking about the Kingdom of God in which He and He alone is King (Mark 1:14,15).

Why am I making so much of this? Just because people so often forget it. I work in a Department of Evangelism. Many organisations send us tracts and gospel teaching aids. These are designed to help people to evangelise their friends. I have been struck with the fact that so many of these neither begin with the Lord Jesus nor do they have as their main focus the Lord Jesus. It seems to me that often the unique person and the unique ministry of the Lord Jesus are not at the centre of much gospel preaching and writing today. Why is it that we rarely 'gospel' people with any of the *four Gospels*? Why is so much gospel preaching focused on man and his need? Could this be one of the reasons why so much evangelistic preaching today is so powerless to change lives? Because it is not God's gospel!? Because it is not the gospel which is "the power of God to salvation" (Romans 1:16)? When God the Father proclaims the gospel—His gospel—then He speaks about the Son and so must we.

(d) The gospel is about a Man/King

"Who as to his human nature was a descendant of David" (verse 3). The two particular features which God wishes us to note about His Son are that He was truly man and that He is truly Son of God. He was truly Man, not just any man. A Man descended from David, a King. In Jesus, God fulfilled His promise to send a king to rule over His people forever. Jesus is undoubtedly Messiah. Matthew begins his Gospel by establishing this, "A record of the genealogy of Jesus Christ the son of David" (Matthew 1:1). Luke is even more explicit in his Gospel. In relating the story of the announcement by the angel Gabriel to the virgin Mary that she would conceive and bear a son, the angel describes the nature of this son as the One who will be "great and will be called the Son of the Most High. The Lord God will give him the throne of his father David, and he will reign over the house of Jacob forever; his kingdom will never end" (Luke 1:33).

There is another significant feature about the fact that Jesus was truly man and which we should note. He *was* born in first century Palestine in Bethlehem—His mother was Mary. Luke, in his Gospel, carefully places this event in its historical setting (Luke 2:1-7). The ministry of John the Baptist and Jesus Himself is set with equal care. Luke tells us "In the fifteenth year of the reign of Tiberius Caesar—when Pontius Pilate was governor of Judea, Herod tetrarch of Galilee, his brother Philip tetrarch of Iturea and Traconitis, and Lysanias tetrarch of Abilene—during the high priesthood of Annas and Caiaphas..." (Luke 3:1,2). This Jesus lived an extraordinary life and died and rose again. Information about Him is obtained in the Gospels—Matthew, Mark, Luke and John.

The gospel is *historical*. The Jesus of history is now seated at the right hand of the Majesty on high. The one who was born in Bethlehem is the Lord of Heaven and earth. He who died on Calvary and rose from the dead will judge the living and the dead. This same Jesus who was descended from David, will return at the end of the age.

Any other experience I may have of Jesus is not to be put forward to men and women as the gospel. My 'experience' of Jesus can and *must* only be understood in terms of God's revelation of Him in the Scriptures. The gospel is anchored in history. It is almost impossible to ask people to commit their lives to Jesus as Lord if they know nothing about this Jesus from the Gospels.

The gospel is about Jesus the Man. It is historical and in that sense it may be thought of as old-fashioned. It certainly isn't new. But novelty has nothing to do with relevance. It isn't irrelevant because it is historical. In fact the very opposite is the case. Because Jesus is truly human He understands me thoroughly. The Jesus of the Gospels is the Man who walked where I walk. He who was tempted as I am, says "come to Me...and I will give you rest" (Matthew 11:28).

In an age which studies little history and puts such a high premium on experience, this aspect of the gospel is often forgotten, yet is the ground of our assurance.

Often I feel as if living the Christian life is too difficult and I am tempted to give it all away. However I remind myself that this is just not on! Jesus Christ really *did* live. He *did* die on the cross and rise again. He *did* ascend into heaven. I am not mistaken. There is no other life to live than the Christian unless I ignore the facts. So I press on with it. The Jesus of my 'experience' cannot sustain me in such a moment of temptation because I am not sure if my experience is real and true. The Jesus of history can and does sustain me in such a moment because there is no doubt about His reality. He really *did* happen. The gospel is historical. It is about the Man who is Messiah.

(e) The gospel is about the powerful Son of God
"...who through the Spirit *(of holiness)* was declared with power to be the Son of God by his resurrection from the dead" (verse 4). Not only is Jesus truly Man but He is

also the Son of God. He had been declared so by the voice from heaven at His baptism and on the mountain when He was transfigured (Mark 1:11; Matthew 17:5), and now Paul tells us that He is "declared with power to be the Son of God", by the fact of His resurrection from the dead. No true gospel can bypass the death and resurrection of Jesus. He died to take the punishment which our sins deserved (1 Corinthians 15:1-3). In these events He shows that He has defeated death (Hebrews 2:14,15), and the power of darkness (John 12:31,32). He has defeated His great enemy and ours (Colossians 2:13-15). He is God's powerful Son who is alive for evermore and consequently is alive now.

The Jesus of history who lived in Palestine, who ate, slept and wept, is the same Jesus who died on the cross and rose again from the dead. By that action He bore our sins and He defeated death. He ascended into heaven and He sent the Holy Spirit into the world. Through His Spirit, Jesus comes to us now in the contemporary situation and makes "all things new" (Revelation 21:5). He who *was* is He who *is*. The historical Jesus is the contemporary Jesus. He is the gospel we preach.

(f) The gospel—Jesus Christ is Lord
"Jesus Christ our Lord" (verse 4). This brings us to the heart of the gospel message.

God the Father has declared His Son, Jesus Christ to be Lord of heaven and earth. After His death and resurrection, Jesus explains to the apostles that "all authority in heaven and on earth has been given to me" (Matthew 28:18). This had special significance since earlier, Jesus had referred to the Father as "Lord of heaven and earth" (Matthew 11:25). Since His death and resurrection, that title is now equally applicable to Jesus. *He* is Lord of heaven and earth. This simple phrase seems to be the clearest and simplest statement of the gospel message.

It is in essence what John the Baptist is saying when he calls on men and women to recognise that "the kingdom of heaven is near" (Matthew 3:2). It is near because the coming King is near. Jesus is that King. His Kingdom is not confined to Israel. All authority in heaven and on earth has been given to Him.

That is what the Father is saying to us. Jesus has had the "name which is above every name" conferred upon Him (Philippians 2:9). He has been enthroned in heaven (Hebrews 1:3). Paul reminds the Romans that salvation is for those who confess with their lips that Jesus is Lord and those who believe in their hearts that God raised Him from the dead (see Romans 10:9).

Our present day trend in evangelistic preaching to separate the Jesus who saved, from the Jesus who rules, is unbiblical; and because it is unbiblical, is totally unhelpful. I cannot have my sins forgiven until I acknowledge Jesus as my King. Our constant use of Revelation 3:20, however helpful the picture of restored fellowship may be, has not ultimately helped us in making clear to people the true nature of our response back to God. 'Opening the door' may or may not convey the idea of surrender to Lordship. It will most certainly do so if the verse is expounded in its context.

Wherever in the Bible we set out to show people the gospel—whenever we are engaging in personal evangelism or speaking to groups large or small, what we must take care to do is to preach God's gospel. God's gospel is about Jesus—the historical/contemporary Jesus—the Jesus who died and rose again taking the punishment our sins deserved—that Jesus who is LORD—the Jesus who is King in the Kingdom of heaven (Matthew 25:31-33; Luke 4:43).

2. What is the response to the gospel?

"...to call people...to the obedience which comes from faith" (verse 5). Once we grasp the fact that the gospel is not a system of doctrine, but the person of Jesus Christ, then we will find that so many other questions fall into place. When we grasp the fact that God has declared His Son Jesus to be Lord of heaven and earth, then we are left with only two alternatives. We can accept it and fall before Him in repentance and faith, or we can reject Him as our rightful ruler and continue in sin.

The Bible makes it clear that all people have rebelled against the rightful rule of Jesus over their lives (Romans

3:12). We all wish to be independent and run our own lives, our own way (Genesis 3:4). We are all under the judgment of God (Romans 1:18; John 3:36), and that is why He calls all people everywhere to repent (Romans 6:15,16; Acts 17:30). Paul is clear as to the response towards which he is preaching. He says that his apostolic ministry is geared to call people "…to the obedience which comes from faith" (verse 5).

Repentance and faith are the only proper responses to God's gospel. God has declared that His Son is Lord. However, I discover through the gospel, that I am a rebel; I don't want Jesus to rule over me. I discover from the gospel that I am under the judgment of God for this rebellion, and there is only one reasonable way to act. I repent of that wilful rebellion in an act of surrender: I acknowledge Jesus as *my* Lord because God has declared Him to be THE Lord. However that alone does not deal with the fact that I have been a rebel. What is to happen about the past? There is only one logical course open to me. I throw myself before God and ask for mercy. I put myself at His mercy and He, in His mercy, forgives me because of the death of His Son Jesus on my behalf.

The true Christian response to the gospel is faith in the Lord Jesus which issues in obedience (repentance). No repentance is true repentance which does not recognise Jesus as Lord over every area of life. No faith is genuine which believes that something extra needs to be added to the death of Jesus to make me acceptable to God. It is not possible to be rescued from the penalty of sin by the death of Jesus while I remain a rebel to Jesus; and equally, I am not acceptable to God if I try to stop rebelling but do not trust in the death of Jesus for the forgiveness of my sins. I may *not* have Jesus as my Saviour if I will not acknowledge Him as my Lord. Jesus is able to save us because He is Lord (Colossians 2:13-15). For too long we have divided the Lord Jesus' twin functions, those of both Saviour and Lord. It may be legitimate to do that for a descriptive purpose, but it is unhelpful to think about the *work* of Jesus apart from the *person* of Jesus.

The modern tendency to ask people to respond to the gospel by 'opening your heart and letting Jesus in', or 'let

Jesus come in and cleanse you from your sin', will leave a person completely open to every possible misunderstanding.

Contrast it with the robust call which must have come from the Apostle Paul to the Thessalonians.

He rejoices that they have turned to God from idols to serve a true and living God (repentance), and were waiting for His Son from heaven, Jesus who delivers from the wrath to come (faith) (1 Thessalonians 1:9,10). Why did they respond like this? *Because it was part of Paul's gospel preaching.* They could not become Christians unless they turned their backs on idolatry in all its forms. But that in itself would be useless unless they placed their trust and confidence in the Jesus who died and rose for them, the Jesus who was coming in judgment and would deliver them from God's anger. There is only one way they could have known this. *Paul told them when he preached the gospel to them.*

Our current lack or clarity at this point has left many people in confusion for years during their Christian life. The way we respond initially to the gospel is the way we are meant to proceed. Repentance and faith are to become our way of life, but they will become so only if we begin that way.

Our churches are graveyards of people who on one hand 'opened the door' but have never repented, they have never come to terms with Christ's Lordship. On the other hand, there are those hard-hearted men and women who in a pseudo-repentance have 'cleaned up their lives' but are affronted by the idea that they need mercy from God and that they are totally unacceptable to God except through the death and resurrection of Jesus.

Paul describes the response for which he preached in these terms—"I have declared to both Jews and Greeks that they must turn to God in repentance and have faith in our Lord Jesus" (Acts 20:21). The promise of salvation is linked with confessing Jesus as Lord and believing that God raised Him from the dead (see Romans 10:9). Have you noticed in the Bible how often we are called upon to respond to Jesus *as* Lord (who will save us), but never as Saviour *without* Lord? (see Luke 2:11; Luke 23:42; Acts

16:31; Romans 10:9; Colossians 2:6; etc.). How is it possible to be a member of the Kingdom of God (or heaven), without acknowledging Jesus as the King?

This matter will be discussed further in chapter three.

3. For whom is the gospel intended?

"...from among all the Gentiles" (verse 5). As we recognise the gospel in terms of Jesus Christ being Lord of heaven and earth, we will immediately see that the extent of the gospel is limitless. Since there is no one who is outside Christ's authority, then all must be told.

If I paddle a canoe up the Amazon, Ganges, Murray or Thames Rivers and ask myself the question "Is Jesus really Lord here?" The answer is clear. He is Lord of heaven and earth, and therefore He is Lord here. Then it is obvious that the inhabitants need to be told this so that they can repent and submit their lives to Christ's authority and thereby put their trust in Him.

I do not question the sincerity of the beliefs of other people, nor that they hold them with tenacity, but the question in the end is "Has God spoken?". Has He really told us the gospel about His Son? Is it true that Jesus is in fact Lord of heaven and earth? Is He seated now on the right hand of the throne of the Majesty on High? Is it a fact that Jesus will return as Judge of all men? If these are indeed facts, then it is inadequate to be a Moslem, or a Buddhist, or a materialist—however sincerely one may hold such beliefs.

A true appreciation of the gospel in terms of Jesus Christ as a person, (and not just as a worker), who lived a perfect life, who died the sin-bearing death, who rose to justify us, who is seated in heaven and who will judge all people, will undoubtedly correct any wrong and inadequate views of both response and the extent of our preaching. As we meditate on Him who is *so very* impressive, it will become a very strong incentive to proclaim Him to all men.

Have you ever noticed in fiction that real people are never completely good or completely bad, but the good and bad are mixed together? Have you noticed that when people are portrayed to us as being completely good, they are never 'real' people, but 'cardboard cut-outs'?

It is impressive that when we read the Gospels, the Jesus we encounter is both completely good and still real. He is at one and the same time thoroughly good and thoroughly believable. The Gospel writers have given us an account of Jesus which is very impressive. We need to re-read the Gospels frequently so that our gospel is a full one and our mental picture of Jesus is a real one. We need to be gripped with the wonder of *who Jesus is* as well as by *what Jesus did*.

It can be argued that what I have said is a Pauline way of looking at the gospel. But what of the gospel which Jesus preached? His gospel centred on the Kingdom of God. Are the two gospels basically different? If they are not, then what is the relationship between the 'gospel of the death and resurrection of Jesus for the forgiveness of sins' as Paul preaches it (1 Corinthians 15:1-3), and the 'gospel of the Kingdom of God' as Jesus preaches it (Mark 1:14,15)?

This is the subject of the next chapter...

CHAPTER THREE

The Gospel and the Kingdom of God

To understand the gospel clearly is the real key to understanding evangelism. If a person is uncertain about the gospel, then he will not be able to engage in evangelism with any confidence. When Jesus preached the gospel He did so in terms of the Kingdom of God (Mark 1:14,15). Paul did it in terms of the death and resurrection of Jesus for the forgiveness of sins (1 Corinthians 15:1-3). Those people who favour the former tend to stress that change in life style is the mark of believing the gospel. Those who favour the latter emphasise that the gospel is about having our sins forgiven. There are questions which need to be resolved if we are to know with any certainty if our gospel is indeed God's gospel. What is the relationship between the gospel of Jesus and the gospel of Paul? Are they the same? Do they interrelate? Or are they alternatives which can be used as circumstances dictate? Was the gospel of the Kingdom for the first century alone? Was it superseded by the Apostle's gospel after Jesus had risen from the dead?

Jesus' theme: the Kingdom of God

The Kingdom of God was a great theme of Jesus' preaching. Mark tells us that Jesus began His preaching by saying, "The time has come. The kingdom of God is near. Repent and believe the good news" (Mark 1:14). Luke tells us that this preaching was so important that Jesus would not be deflected from it. On one occasion when the crowd pressed upon Him for healing He left them with the words, "I must preach the good news of the kingdom of God to the other towns also, because that is why I was sent" (Luke 4:43). Jesus explained to Nicodemus that the Kingdom of God is so significant, it cannot be recognised or entered except by supernatural means. "Unless a man is born again, he cannot see the kingdom of God" (John 3:3). When asked by Pilate if He were indeed a king, Jesus replied, "My kingdom is not of this world. If it were, my servants would fight to prevent my arrest by the Jews. But now my kingdom is from another place" (John 18:36). So important was the Kingdom that a person was to seek it as the highest priority. It was what life was really all about. Seeking it carried the promise of God's providential care (Matthew 6:33). These are but a few of the many references made by Jesus to show that it was a major theme of His preaching.

Not only was it the theme of Jesus' preaching but He believed that the Kingdom of God had arrived with His own arrival. He was the King. He was in fact that 'Son of David' who would reign over God's people in an ever-lasting Kingdom (Isaiah 9:7).

On one occasion when Jesus was casting out demons (Luke 11:14ff), the Pharisees claimed that He was able to perform this by his league with Beelzebub, the prince of demons. Jesus' response to this is important. He claimed that such power could not and would not be given by Beelzebub to destroy himself. Jesus' claim is that He has Himself, by the power of God, confronted the kingdom of darkness and overpowered it. That fact should have caused them to recognise that God's Kingly rule, the Kingdom of God, had arrived in the person of Himself, "If I drove out demons by the finger of God, then the kingdom of God has come to you" (Luke 11:20). In the ministry of Jesus the proclaiming of the Kingdom of God in word and action was the same as proclaiming the gospel. To recognise Him as King was to recognise the gospel. To believe in Him as King was to inherit eternal life (Luke 23:42,43).

Paul's theme: the Kingdom of God

It has sometimes been argued that the gospel which Paul preached was different from that of Jesus. Luke would not agree with this. In his two volumes 'The Gospel of Luke' and 'The Acts of the Apostles', Luke shows how both Jesus and Paul preached the gospel of the Kingdom. We have already seen the high priority which Jesus put on this preaching (Luke 4:43), and it was also the theme of Paul's preaching.

When he was returning to Jerusalem at the end of the final missionary journey, Paul came to Miletus and sent for the elders of Ephesus. Paul's long farewell to them is recorded for us (Acts 20:17-36). In it Paul gives a summary of his ministry with them. He tells how he did not hesitate to declare to them "the whole will of God" (Acts 20:27). He reminds them that he urged all people both publicly and privately to repent and believe on the Lord Jesus (Acts 20:20,21). But when he wishes to summarise his preaching ministry in a word, he does it in terms of the Kingdom. He says, "Now I know that none of you among whom I have gone about preaching the kingdom will ever see me again" (Acts 20:25). It was a short-hand expression for the gospel. In Paul's thinking to "declare to both Jews and Greeks that they must turn to God in repentance and have faith in our Lord Jesus" (Acts 20:21), was 'preaching the kingdom'.

In Luke's mind the gospel Paul preached was the same gospel which Jesus preached; they both proclaimed the Kingdom of God. Luke describes Paul's imprisonment at Rome, and in doing so makes two further references to his preaching. The Jewish leaders at Rome came to hear Paul explain about the new 'sect'. They turned out in large numbers. "From morning till evening he explained and declared to them the kingdom of God and tried to convince them about Jesus from the law of Moses and from the Prophets" (Acts 28:23). Finally Luke makes a summary statement to conclude his book, "For two whole years Paul stayed there in his own rented house and welcomed all who came to see him. Boldly and without hindrance he preached the kingdom of God and taught about the Lord Jesus Christ" (Acts 28:30,31).

When we read Paul's letters the gospel is often stated in different terms. The death and resurrection of Jesus for the forgiveness of sins become prominent (1 Corinthians

15:1-5; Colossians 2:11-15). And again the question springs to mind: 'What is the relationship between the preaching of the gospel of the Kingdom of God and that expressed in terms of the death and resurrection of Jesus?' What has the death of Jesus to do with God establishing His rule forever in the person of Jesus?

Jesus' teaching: the cross and the Kingdom

In Jesus' teaching there is an indispensable connection between the establishing of His Kingly rule, and the defeat of Satan which is brought about by His death and resurrection. The incident, already described, about Jesus casting out the demon from the dumb man, and the ensuing conversation, provide us with an important insight into this question. The Jews accused Jesus of being able to perform the miracle by Beelzebub the prince of the demons. Jesus replied that He had done it by God and that it showed that God's Kingdom had arrived and was in their midst. He then proceeded to an interesting parable, "When a strong man, fully armed, guards his own house, his possessions are safe. But when someone stronger attacks and overpowers him, he takes away the armour in which the man trusted and divides up the spoils" (Luke 11:21,22). Rather than being able to do this miracle by satanic powers, Jesus declared that He was doing the absolute opposite. He was in fact storming the strongholds of Satan and spoiling them. He was challenging this 'ruler of darkness' that He might defeat him forever and be seen to be the undoubted King. If you defeat your greatest enemy who is there left to defeat?

This ultimate victory Jesus saw to be accomplished through His death. John, in his Gospel (John 12:21-33), tells of the incident when the Greeks came to Philip with the request, "Sir, we would see Jesus". Jesus was moved by this event. "The hour has come for the Son of Man to be glorified," He said. He began to speak about a seed going into the ground and dying so that it might spring to life and grow. It is a reference to His own death and resurrection. The discourse climaxes with Jesus calling on the Father to glorify His name. A voice is heard from heaven, "I have glorified it and I will glorify it again" (John 12:28). There is some discussion as to whether it was in fact a voice or thunder. Jesus assured them with the words, "This voice was for your benefit, not mine. Now is the judgment on this world; now the prince of this world will be driven out. But I, when I am lifted up from the earth, will draw all men to myself" (John 12:30-32). John makes the comment, "He said this to show the kind of death he was going to die" (John 12:33).

The defeat of Satan (the prince of this world) and the death of Jesus are closely connected. Jesus understood that His Kingly rule would be established through His death and resurrection, because it was a 'ransom for many' (Matthew 20:28), and the means whereby our sins could be forgiven (Matthew 26:28). These two aspects must not be separated as if one could take place without the other. Jesus' death is a death in sin-bearing. He is the 'lamb' of God who bears away the sin of the world (John 1:29). In doing this He is able to set us free from our slavery to sin and Satan, and in freeing us it is obvious that He has defeated His great enemy and ours. He has 'overpowered him' (Luke 11:22) and is undisputed Lord. When He has defeated His greatest enemy there is none other left to challenge His authority. It is a consequence of His sin-bearing death and resurrection that Jesus is able to say, "All authority in heaven and on earth has been given to me" (Matthew 28:18).

Paul's teaching: the death of Jesus and His Lordship

The connection between the death of Jesus and His defeat of Satan is even more clearly described by Paul. In his letter to the Colossians he explains that Christ's death is the means whereby we can be completely forgiven. He pictures all our debts being nailed to the cross of Christ and goes on to explain "and having disarmed the powers and authorities, he made a public spectacle of them, triumphing over them by the cross" (Colossians 2:15).

It is a graphic illustration. When Roman generals came home to Rome in triumph they would ride in their chariots to which were chained the rulers of the cities and countries they had conquered. It said in an unmistakable way to even the smallest child in Rome, "So great is the mighty power of Rome that we turn the rulers of our enemies into our slaves". It was the mark of absolute supremacy. Paul picks out the metaphor as if to say 'Do you understand the full import of your sins being forgiven? The cross of Jesus is so significant that it is a triumphant procession to which the principalities and powers have been chained to show that they are utterly defeated'.

This idea is again spelt out in the Epistle to the Hebrews. Jesus' death is described as the means by which He would "destroy him who holds the power of death— that is, the devil—and free those, who all their lives, were held in slavery by their fear of death" (Hebrews 2:14,15).

Saviour and Lord: not one without the other

The immediate implication of the 'Kingdom of God' gospel should not be lost. Jesus is able to save us from sin and death because of His overthrow and defeat of Satan. He is able to save because He is Lord. Consequently it is not possible to accept Jesus as Saviour and *not* as Lord since He saved by *being* Lord.

The Bible may separate these functions of Jesus to describe them but they are inseparable when applied to mankind. That is why the true response of a person to Christ is a genuine repentance which involves recognising Jesus as true King in God's world and thus seeking to live under His authority. Great damage has been done by encouraging people to invite Jesus into their lives as the One who will save them and forgive them without any real call to repent of an independent attitude towards Jesus' right to be Lord.

Notice the way the Gospel writer will not divide these two aspects of Jesus' ministry. Matthew begins his Gospel with the words "a record of...Jesus Christ the son of David...and Jesse the father of King David" (Matthew 1:1,6). We are in no doubt that Jesus is King. When the angel comes to Joseph in a dream he is told that the child to be born is to be called "Jesus, because he will save his people from their sins" (Matthew 1:21). We are in no doubt that the King is the Saviour.

This was always the way God envisaged His kings to be. When Samuel anointed Saul King over Israel he did so with the words, "You will reign over the Lord's people and save them from the power of their enemies round about" (1 Samuel 10:1*).

At Caesarea Philippi when Peter makes his marvellous confession, "You are the Christ, the Son of the living God", Jesus teaches the disciples that He will go up to Jerusalem to die and to rise again (Matthew 16:16-28). The King is one who suffers and dies and rises again.

When James and John ask if they have the places of privilege when Jesus comes into His Kingdom, Jesus explains that the essence of the Kingdom is in service to others and that in particular it is in His giving His life a ransom for many (Matthew 20:28). It is because "all authority in heaven and on earth" has been given to Jesus that the nations have to be discipled (Matthew 28:18,19). When the angel announced the gospel to the shepherds on the hillsides around Bethlehem it was in the words "I bring you good news of great joy that will be for all the people. Today in the town of David a Saviour has been born to you; he is Christ the Lord" (Luke 2:10,11). The *Saviour* is the *Lord*. They knew nothing of one without the other—neither must we in our preaching. Nowhere does the Bible call on us to receive Jesus *only* as Saviour. We are invited to trust Him and to receive Him (John 1:12).

In John's Gospel 'to receive' Jesus means to believe on His name, which means to believe on Him as God. This is to recognise 'the Word' of whom John has been speaking, and to act accordingly. But what is the way in which John has spoken about Jesus?

John begins his Gospel by reminding us that Jesus, the *Word*, was in the beginning with God, and was in fact, God. All things were created by Him and He is light and life (John 1:1-5). He goes on to say that Jesus came to His

*Hebrew; Septuagint and Vulgate.

own people the Jews, and they rejected Him. They did not recognise Him as the *Word*, as he is described by John, but nonetheless we are assured by John that to all who receive Jesus (the *Word*), He will give the authority to become the children of God. To receive Him means to recognise Him to be the *Word* and to act accordingly. It is another way of speaking about repentance, and it is important when using John's Gospel in evangelism to remember that he does not use the word 'repentance' at all.

This is also contained in the idea of 'believing in the name of the Son' (John 1:12), or 'believing on the Son' (John 3:36). It is worth noting that in John's Gospel the terms 'obey' and 'believe' are often synonyms (John 3:36). It is not possible to believe and not obey, or to obey and not believe.

The gospel: good for all times?
When the gospel is understood in terms of the Lordship of Christ through His sin-bearing death and resurrection, it will be clear that this message is appropriate for all people at all times irrespective of their backgrounds. Whether I am a believer or an unbeliever will not change the message. When as a believer I hear the gospel that Jesus is Lord, I am encouraged to continue in repentance and faith since my obedience is not perfect in this life. I will always be called to renewed commitment. If an unbeliever hears the gospel that Jesus is Lord, that too is a call to a life of repentance and faith. There is no message for the unbeliever which is not appropriate for the believer.

This truth relieves us of having to engage in spiritual diagnosis. Whether the person before me is a believer or an unbeliever I still have *one* gospel and that gospel is equally applicable.

Because of this we are urged not only to believe the gospel but to live by the gospel. The way we begin in the Christian life is the way we continue, "...just as you received Christ Jesus as Lord, continue to live in him..." (Colossians 2:6). There is no thought in the Bible of a two-stage coming to Christ when we receive Jesus as Saviour and later acknowledge Him as Lord. It may prove that many have been given false assurance of sins forgiven but who were never truly born-again, and in whose lives no new work of repentance and faith took place. It is the new life under the authority of Jesus, as well as trusting in the work of Jesus, which assures us that we are truly God's children, members of the Kingdom (1 John 3:4-6; 3:14, 4:12).

When Paul summarises his gospel he can do it either by saying "For we do not preach ourselves, but Jesus Christ as Lord" (2 Corinthians 4:5), or by the phrase "I have gone about preaching the kingdom" (Acts 20:25), or "Now, brothers, I want to remind you of the gospel I preached to you...that Christ died for our sins according to the Scriptures, that he was buried, that he was raised on the third day..." (1 Corinthians 15:1,3,4). These are all understood to be interlocking terms. Each is understood in the framework of the others.

Let us be done with the truncated gospel which presents only part of the true person and work of Jesus. Praise God He is both Saviour and Lord. He is able to effect a permanent salvation for us.

The victory without atonement?

If the inter-relationship between the victory of the Lord Jesus over Satan and His sin-bearing death are not recognised, it is possible to preach one aspect as if the other did not exist. When this happens the response which people will make will not be that of repentance *and* faith.

What will happen if I emphasise the victory of Jesus but neglect the sin-bearing aspect of His death? Calvary will be seen only as a victory. Jesus will be declared as King. People will try to respond by reforming their lives, seeking to live under the rule of Jesus. They will believe that their new 'reformed' life will win acceptance with God. To try and come to God without trusting in Jesus' death as the means whereby our sins are forgiven is to disregard what God says about the death of His Son (1

John 1:7). The Kingly rule of Jesus is established by His sin-bearing death. To acknowledge Jesus as Lord and not to trust Him as Saviour from the penalty of sin is to misunderstand the gospel.

Atonement without the victory?

However, it is possible to err in the other direction. It is possible to emphasise the sin-bearing act of Jesus as if His Kingly rule were quite independent of it. People will respond to this by believing that their sins can be forgiven and that they will be acceptable to God because of the death of Jesus, whether they truly repent and acknowledge Jesus as Lord or not. To respond like this is to ignore what God says (Romans 10:9). To trust Jesus as Saviour and not acknowledge Him as Lord is to misunderstand the gospel.

Whenever the gospel is preached whether in terms of the 'Kingdom of God' or of the 'death of Jesus for the forgiveness of sins' both ideas must be conveyed. One is not to be understood without the other. They are not alternative or opposing 'gospels'. They are aspects of the same gospel. One without the other leaves the gospel inadequate.

That being so, the next question to ask is, "Whose job is it to preach it?" The apostles, or the evangelists, or every Christian—what does the Bible say?

CHAPTER FOUR

Who Should do the Work of Evangelism?

I was led to Christ by the boy who sat next to me in High School. He was converted during our second year and immediately he began to evangelise me. Although I was a regular churchgoer, it was apparent to him, as indeed it would have been to a casual observer, that I knew nothing about the gospel.

If I had heard the gospel, and I suppose I must have, I certainly had not taken it in. At that time I thought a Christian was someone who went to church and tried to live a good life. I knew that Jesus Christ had come into the world, that He was the Son of God. I knew about His death and resurrection, but I didn't associate those facts with anything in my life. I didn't understand sin in terms of rebellion to the living God whose right it was to run my life. I had no concept of a holy God before whom I would one day give an account of my life. I just went to church, sang in the choir and generally thought it was good fun.

A school friend began to 'show' me the gospel. He told it to me himself and he took me to where it was preached. Over the period of some three years, I came to recognise that Jesus was indeed the Son of God and Ruler of the world. I saw myself for what I was, a rebel against God, and I recognised myself to be under His judgment. I came to understand that Jesus Christ had died on the cross to take the punishment which my rebellion deserved, and I turned back to Christ and asked for mercy and forgiveness. I began to trust Him as the only way to get right with God and I tried to live a life of obedience.

There were more people involved in this process than

Dick but he was the driving force. I had been converted, not presumably by professionals, but by an amateur. It was a truly 'lay' movement. Consequently I assumed that this was the way it should be.

Since I had been led to Christ by an ordinary Christian it encouraged me to try to do the same. At the church I went to I was taught that in the Great Commission recorded in Matthew 28:18, Christ had commissioned all Christians to do the work of evangelism, and so we all should do it.

As time went by I discovered two things which threw doubt on that idea. The first one was that the Great Commission was given to the apostles and was not automatically applicable to all Christians even at that time. The second was that since Christ had given evangelists as a gift to the church (Ephesians 4:11), they were the ones whose role it was to do this work. My role was to support them with my prayers, encouragement and gifts. I began to think that evangelism was for the professional and not a 'lay' movement after all.

I have come to see that there is substance in both these ideas yet I am convinced that the Bible expects *all* Christians to be actively engaged in evangelism directly and personally, not vicariously through the apostles and evangelists or the Church.

The apostles only?
In Matthew's Gospel, the Great Commission "All authority in heaven and on earth has been given to me. Therefore go and make disciples of all nations", is given to the "eleven disciples" (Matthew 28:16-18). In Luke's Gospel this group is extended to "the eleven and *those with them*" (Luke 24:33). He tells us that the risen Christ appeared to them with this announcement, "...The Christ will suffer and rise from the dead on the third day, and repentance and forgiveness of sins will be preached in his name to all nations, beginning at Jerusalem. You are witnesses of these things" (Luke 24:46-48). Although the group of people who are told this are now the 'extended eleven' they are not explicitly commanded to

do the work. In John's Gospel, it is again the apostles for whom Christ prays in His High-Priestly prayer. To them He has given the words from the Father which they will preach that others may believe (John 17:6-20).

Luke, the author of Acts, tells us that it was to the apostles that Jesus gave the command, "Do not leave Jerusalem, but wait for the gift my Father promised" (Acts 1:2-4). It appears as if it is to the apostles that the command is given, "...But you will receive power when the Holy Spirit comes on you; and you will be my witnesses in Jerusalem, and in all Judea and Samaria, and to the ends of the earth" (Acts 1:8). There is little doubt that the term 'witness' here refers to those who witnessed Jesus alive from the dead (Acts 1:22; 2:32; 5:32; 13:31). It does not mean, as is so often used today, an act of personal testimony however valuable that is.

It is because of these facts that some have concluded that the work of evangelism was primarily that of the apostles and then of the evangelists whose role it still is. They argue that all are obligated to live the Christian life but since *all* are obviously not evangelists, then all do not need to engage in this activity. But who are the evangelists?

The elusive evangelist

In Ephesians 4:11, Paul tells us that the ascended Christ gave gifts to His Church. Among these are 'evangelists'. Knowing what their role was, presents us with no small difficulty. This arises because we hardly know anything about them. There are only three references to them in the New Testament. We know they are (or were), the gift of the victorious Christ to the Church (Ephesians 4:11). We know that Philip was one (Acts 21:8), and that Timothy is told to do the work of an evangelist and to fulfil his ministry (2 Timothy 4:5)! Perhaps he thought he didn't have the gift, like so many ministers today, or perhaps he was just forgetful, like us all. It would be interesting to ponder whether he is called upon to do this work because he is an elder, or a teacher of scripture, or because Paul recognised this gift in him.

These three references do not give us a really clear picture of the role of the evangelist. He may have been an itinerant preacher of the gospel—or just someone gifted in leading people to Christ. He may have been a New Testament extension of the Old Testament prophet. We just don't know. But the question still remains that if some are evangelists then is it their job to preach the gospel and be responsible for the work of evangelism rather than every Christian? I remember well when this idea first came to us. It was welcomed with open arms. Everyone immediately discovered they didn't have to bother unless they were 'evangelists'. They were equally certain that none of them was! It was the only time in the history of our country when we were left with no 'evangelists'—(except me, and I had to because I was the Director of the Department of Evangelism!). What a great foolishness it all was.

There is a special gift of the evangelist as there is a special gift of faith (1 Corinthians 12:9) but that doesn't mean all of us shouldn't evangelise, any more than it means we don't all need to exercise faith.

Where then does the Bible say it is the job of *all* Christians?

To declare the mighty deeds of God

The people of God are described in 1 Peter in terms taken directly from the Old Testament. He says, "You are a chosen people, a royal priesthood, a holy nation, a people belonging to God, that you may declare the praises of him who called you out of darkness into his wonderful light. Once you were not a people, but now you are the people of God; once you had not received mercy, but now you have received mercy" (1 Peter 2:9,10). Two matters are apparent from this:

First: God's people are special people. They are specially chosen by Him, and as such, cannot be ordinary. They are not unimportant to Him. They shouldn't be to us. Had the choice of who would be Christians been left to us we may have chosen differently, which only shows how much we are unlike God! He loves them. We should love them.

Second: God's People have a special task. Their job is to declare the praises of God. These praises are all associated with the work of salvation—darkness to light—'no people' to God's people—wrath to mercy.

To whom is this declaration made?
It could be a declaration to each other in praise of the God who saves, as in Revelation 7:10 where the multitude in heaven cry in a loud voice, "Salvation belongs to our God, who sits on the throne, and to the Lamb". It could be a declaration to the "rulers and authorities in the heavenly realms" of God's great wisdom (Ephesians 3:10). However, since God's people are here described in Old Testament terms which referred to Israel (Isaiah 43:20; Exodus 19:6), there can be no doubt that the declaration is to be made to the 'nations' (Isaiah 49:1) to whom Israel is called to witness (Mark 11:17, Isaiah 56:6,7). The declaration of God's mighty deeds in salvation is to be made known to those who are not yet Christian. All Christians belong to the people whose purpose is to "declare the mighty deeds of God". This scripture does not necessarily mean that the individual has to engage personally in evangelism. It does mean, however, that we all belong to a people whose purpose is to 'declare the mighty deeds of God" (Psalms 9:9; 96:3; 145:4; 1 Peter 2:9).

Living or speaking?
The Apostle Peter in his letter continues to show that living the Christian life is one of the ways he envisages this great declaration to be made. He immediately directs them in aspects of Christian living (1 Peter 2:11-5:11). Many say "I don't need to tell people about Jesus, I live the Christian life and people will see Jesus in me and be drawn to Him". There is a very valuable truth in this but it is not the whole picture. Godly living is a top priority of all Christians (Romans 8:29). However, the godly life is at best ambiguous. People will certainly recognise *that* a Christian is different if he lives the Christian life. They will not, however, be able to work out *why* he is different.

Having said that, I do not want to underestimate the power of the godly life in its effect. Only this week I heard of a Christian undergraduate who was lectured in one of his courses by a Jewish lecturer. In connection with this course, he had been on several weekend excursions with a group led by this lecturer. His sensitivity and thoughtfulness to see that this Jewish man was not inconvenienced either in religious observances or with available food had been noticed and appreciated by the lecturer. On enquiry he discovered the boy was a Christian. He now recognised that there are Christians and 'Christians'— true ones and others. From one point of view it is a small matter but from another it is a massive one. The undergraduate should behave with love whether it is noticed or not. He should do it whether it has evangelistic significance or not. He should love because God loves. Yet love is very hard to hide and has a habit of being recognised.

From one point of view that behaviour does "declare the praises of him who called you out of darkness..." (1 Peter 2:9). In a godly community, well instructed in the Bible which associates goodness with God, the declaration is clear. In others it remains ambiguous. It is true that goodness and kindness cannot be hidden. Love and gentleness will be appreciated, but God will hardly ever be seen to be the cause of these unless some explanation is given. That explanation must be the gospel.

In the Sermon on the Mount, Jesus tells us "let your light shine before men, that they may see your good works and praise your Father in heaven" (Matthew 5:16). I have found that godly behaviour is hardly ever associated with God. When people 'let their light shine before men', God is not necessarily glorified. What usually happens is that they themselves are glorified. "What a kind person you are" is the reaction. God is not seen to be the cause or the purpose of the behaviour. If it is ever given religious significance it is always in terms of "I'm sure you will go to heaven". The gospel needs to be *heard* as well as *seen* in action so that God will indeed be glorified. The hearing and the seeing make a very powerful combination.

It is because of this that Peter in this Epistle goes on to tell the Christians "Always be prepared to give the reason for the hope that you have" (1 Peter 3:15).

Always be prepared

We belong to the people who are to live for the praise of God's glory. We are all to be ready to give a reason for the hope that is within us. We are to be ready at any time to do this. This cannot mean anything less than to be ready to make a clear statement of the gospel. The Apostle Peter expects all Christians to be able and ready to make a defence for their faith.

It is envisaged that every Christian knows and can articulate the gospel. He should know it in a clear and specific form so that he is able to persuade others. None is exempt from this. All are to be prepared for such an eventuality. I will show later that it is the role of the minister to see that his people are competent to do this. It is part of his pastoral teaching duty. However, he will not be able to discharge this unless he himself does it also.

It is one thing to be ready and equipped to give a defence for the gospel, and to do so when called upon, but it is another to actively engage in a way of life which looks for opportunities to tell people the gospel. One is passive, the other is active. One is defensive, the other is offensive. The former waits for others to take the initiative, the latter is trying regularly to initiate conversation which will lead to the gospel. Can it be argued that the latter is the New Testament norm? I believe it can.

Meat offered to idols

Paul, in the first letter to the Corinthians, addressed himself to many problems in that early church. Not the least of which was the problem of meat offered to idols and attending feasts in idol temples. This is discussed at length (1 Corinthians 8:1 to 11:1) and whilst I do not want to go into detail of the whole argument, I do want to draw attention to a clear underlying principle, that the

Christian person does everything he can to bring the gospel to as many people as possible.

In Corinth the church members were acting in unloving ways towards each other and from purely selfish motives. Paul tells them the Christian way is the opposite to this. He reminds them he never insisted on his rights when he was with them (1 Corinthians 9:1-12), indeed he purposely pursued a lifestyle which made it easy for people to hear and receive the gospel (1 Corinthians 9:13-18). He reaches a climax with the statement

"Though I am free and belong to no man, I make myself a slave to everyone, to win as many as possible. To the Jews I became like a Jew, to win the Jews. To those under the law I became like one under the law...so as to win those under the law. To those not having the law I became like one not having the law...so as to win those not having the law. To the weak I became weak, to win the weak. I have become all things to all men so that by all possible means I might save some" (1 Corinthians 9:19-22).

Paul's flexibility and complete identification is directed towards the salvation of the maximum number of people. Indeed his whole life is geared to this end. His argument on the subject of meat offered to idols comes to a conclusion where the same principle is restated, "Do not cause anyone to stumble, whether Jews, Greeks or the church of God—even as I try to please everybody in every way. For I am not seeking my own good but the good of many, so that they may be saved" (1 Corinthians 10:32,33).

He reiterates his life principle. It is a 'sacrificial—flexible—identification' with all men *in order* that they may come to salvation. It is evangelistic in its thrust. It might be thought that this attitude existed in Paul because of his special call to be an apostle to the Gentiles (Acts 26:15-18) and was different for all Christians. However, Paul immediately explains to the Corinthians that he obtained this attitude from the Lord Jesus and he calls on them to copy him as he in his turn is copying the

Lord Jesus, "Be imitators of me, as I am of Christ" (1 Corinthians 11:1; RSV).

That attitude of life which 'seeks and saves the lost' is to be the attitude of all Christians. That self-sacrificing spirit of the One who "...though he was rich, yet for your sakes he became poor", is to be the spirit of all Christians. That heart full of compassion seen in the One who when He looked on the crowds saw them "harassed and helpless, like sheep without a shepherd" (Matthew 9:36), is to be the heart of all Christians. It is clear that it is the joyous task, as well as the solemn responsibility, of all Christians to actively seek the salvation of people around them. We are to do this by living Christianly and by telling the gospel as opportunity arises.

Since we all find this work hard we need to be strongly motivated from the Bible and we need to encourage ourselves and our Christian friends about what it says. What then are the reasons the Bible gives?

CHAPTER FIVE

Why Should we Bother?

I always thought that there was something wrong with me because I found evangelism so difficult—especially on a one-to-one basis. I thought that other Christians found it easy, and I was hardly ever brave enough to admit how I really felt. It was years before I came to understand that we all find evangelism hard. Consequently we need to be clear in our minds that God *does* want us to be actively engaged in this work. Thankfully, the Bible gives us clear reasons, and I have listed five of them:
1. The purpose of the world in which we live
2. The character of God
3. The seriousness of life
4. The nature of the gospel
5. The purpose of man

1. The purpose of the world in which we live
What kind of world is ours? At any given moment in history it is impossible to know what God is doing in His world unless He tells us. Sometimes identical incidents from our point of view have very different underlying reasons when God explains them. He uses them for different purposes.

This is demonstrated in two events. One in Job's life and the other in the invasion of Judah by Assyria. The Chaldeans swept in and stole Job's property (Job 1:17). The Assyrians, years later, do exactly the same to Judah (Isaiah 10:5-7). Both appear to be identical, both peoples are powerful, both are greedy and both take what is not theirs. Yet when God explains these historical events, we are given a completely different perspective.

In the case of Job, God allows the incidents so that Job will come to know Him at greater depth (Job 42:1-6). However, the Assyrian invasion of Judah is quite different. This is a direct punishment because of the disobedience of God's people (Isaiah 10:5-7).

We cannot interpret any historical event without an explanation from God, but we do know that God is the master of history and that His ultimate purposes for it will be fulfilled. This purpose is clearly stated. Paul tells us that God has "made known to us the mystery of his will according to his good pleasure, which he purposed in Christ, to be put into effect when the times will have reached their fulfilment—to bring all things in heaven and on earth together under one head, even Christ" (Ephesians 1:9,10). God's purpose is that everything in creation will acknowledge that Jesus is Lord (Philippians 2:10,11).

Jesus is at the centre of all God's purposes (Colossians 1:16). Since God has disclosed *His* purpose for the world, the Christians' aim should exactly coincide with His. We should be calling on men and women to recognise that God exists and that Jesus is Lord and we should act accordingly. In other words we should tell them the gospel.

2. The character of God

What kind of a god is God? Again and again we are reminded that God longs for men and women to turn back to Him in repentance. He tells us that He has no pleasure in the death of the wicked. He longed that they will return to a loving relationship of trust with Him (Ezekiel 33:11). He grieves over men's hardness of heart (Luke 19:41-44). He delays the final judgment so that people may repent (2 Peter 3:8,9).

Matthew describes the attitude of Jesus in this way. "When he saw the crowds, he had compassion on them, because they were harassed and helpless, like sheep without a shepherd. Then he said to his disciples, "The harvest is plentiful but the workers are few. Ask the Lord of the harvest, therefore, to send out workers into his harvest field'" (Matthew 9:36-38).

The true disciple of Jesus should be growing like his Lord. He should love the things Jesus loves and do the things Jesus did. This is really what being godly is all about. Whenever we see Jesus in a given situation we know how we should behave in a similar situation. We know exactly how Jesus reacted when He saw the crowds. His heart welled up with compassion and that compassion resulted in action. "Ask (pray) the Lord of the harvest." Do you do this? When we look around us in our world we should be moved with pity. 'Harassed and helpless' is a very apt description of men and women apart from Christ.

I remember many years ago speaking with a young man who was engaged in full time student evangelism in the university of Madras. He spent a long time explaining to me the many problems he was encountering. At the end of that meeting we spent some time praying together. During this prayer he dissolved into terrible sobbing. Being Anglo-saxon, I was embarrassed, he was not. With tears rolling down his cheeks he said, "There are times when I think my heart will break—so few of my countrymen turn back to Christ". As I went back to my hotel I thought that he was behaving just like his Lord who "As He approached Jerusalem and saw the city, he wept over it and said, 'If you, even you, had only known on this day what would bring you peace—but now it is hidden from your eyes'" (Luke 19:41,42).

God's concern of love issued in action. It was not passive. "This is how God showed his love among us: He sent his one and only Son into the world that we might live through him" (1 John 4:9). The compassion of the Lord Jesus was not weak and sentimental but strong and active. It was not passive. He loved us and gave Himself for us (Galatians 2:20). Our concern cannot be real if it remains passive. It must issue in action.

The first action should be that of prayer. We are to pray for an increase of labourers, and if we do that regularly and consistently, we will soon realise that we could be the answer to our own prayer. We can increase the labourers by one!

As well as prayer, we will seek ways to tell people of the

Good Shepherd who leads, cares for the flock and who laid down His life for them (John 10:1-11). Paul, the apostle, echoes this same sentiment in these words—"I have great sorrow and unceasing anguish in my heart. For I could wish that I myself were cursed and cut off from Christ for the sake of my brothers, those of my own race, the people of Israel" (Romans 9:2-4). It is an extraordinary statement! He would be prepared to forfeit his salvation if only his countrymen would turn to Christ!

God's purpose in creating us was that we should reflect His image (Genesis 1:26). His purpose in calling us back to Himself is so that we should reflect Christ's image (Romans 8:29). God has declared his love for sinful men (John 3:16). He longs that they will repent. Consequently we are not in the dark about how we should react to those outside of Christ. Most of us need a new work of the Holy Spirit within us to soften our hard hearts and cause us to grow more and more like Jesus in this respect. Why not pray that He will do that for you right now?

3. The seriousness of life

What happens in the end? As well as declaring His plan for the world, God has graciously warned mankind of the coming judgment (Hebrews 9:27). He will not let rebellion against Christ's rule continue indefinitely and because of that He commands all people everywhere to repent. The Father has fixed the day and has appointed the Son as judge (Acts 17:30; John 5:22). The Son warns us of the seriousness of the judgment and of hell (Matthew 10:28; 11:21; 25:31-46; Mark 9:47; John 3:36). Jesus warns us because He loves us. God will not allow goodness and badness to flourish side by side for ever. He, whose throne is built on justice and righteousness, will see that righteousness prevails. That is why sin must, and will be punished. Not only are we reminded of the fact of judgment but also of the terrible consequences of arriving at that day unprepared.

Paul describes the basis and results of judgment to the Thessalonians. They were under strong persecution.

Paul assures them that this condition will not last forever. Christ Himself will right all wrongs. He encourages them not to give up. "All this is evidence that God's judgment is right, and as a result you will be counted worthy of the kingdom of God, for which you are suffering. God is just: He will pay back trouble to those who trouble you and give relief to you who are troubled, and to us as well. This will happen when the Lord Jesus is revealed from heaven in blazing fire with his powerful angels. He will punish those who do not know God and do not obey the gospel of our Lord Jesus. They will be punished with everlasting destruction and shut out from the presence of the Lord and from the majesty of his power on the day when he comes to be glorified in his holy people and to be marvelled at among all those who have believed" (2 Thessalonians 1:5-10).

Notice the basis for the judgment is relationship with God and obedience to the gospel. However, what is shattering is the description of hell. It is an existence of exclusion from God. It is to experience the loss of everything valuable.

Several years ago I was conducting an evangelistic mission in a small village in northern New South Wales. One afternoon whilst visiting and inviting people to attend the meetings, I asked a very old man sitting on a verandah if he would like to come. "I'm too old for that", he said. So I decided that if he wasn't coming to the meeting, the meeting would come to him.

As I sat on the verandah and chatted to him, I steered the conversation towards a discussion on life and death. I asked him if he was ready for death when it should come. He laughed!

"Do you think I will go to hell?"

"Everyone whose sins are unforgiven will go to hell."

"Well" said he, "there'll be a lot of my mates there."

"No, there will be no mates because there will be no friendship. People, but not friends."

We continued our discussion, and he at least did not leave this earth without having heard a clear presentation of the gospel.

To be apart from God is to be apart from everything

good, since *every* good gift comes from above (James 1:17). God gives these good things to believers and unbelievers alike (Matthew 5:45). Love and friendship come from God. People may not believe it or acknowledge this to be so but that does not change the fact. To be excluded from God's presence is to exist without any of the 'good and perfect gifts' which come from Him. To exist without love, kindness, or generosity in the great aloneness, is hell indeed. Hell is a very lonely place.

To be frightened by the prospect of it is to react in exactly the way Jesus tells us to (Luke 23:4,5). It is because of the judgment that God commands us to repent (Acts 17:30). To reject the Son of God and to continue to live that way is to be under God's wrath (John 3:36).

The gospel speaks comfort and hope to those under judgment. Jesus, through His death and resurrection, can rescue us from the coming wrath (1 Thessalonians 1:10). It is not pleasant nor always fashionable to speak about God's anger and hell, but it is a reality, and the Bible doesn't baulk at it. We need to remind ourselves of it. Our nice, kind, gentle, generous, lovable friends who have rejected the gospel are hell bound. It is a strong incentive to take to them the gospel which tells of rescue and forgiveness.

The idea of judgment and punishment is not one which any of us like. We will always be under strong temptation to forget and minimise it. It is part of being a sinful person to do so. The prime temptation is to doubt the reality of judgment. In the Garden of Eden the devil tempted the woman to doubt the fact of judgment by telling her that she would not die, but would in fact become like God (Genesis 3:4,5). That statement was, and still remains, a lie. Our actions have consequences and all temptations to believe the opposite must be resisted. Disbelief in judgment is natural to sinful people, that is why we, as Christians, must resist it.

Many people find it difficult to believe that a loving God will punish people like the Bible says He will. However, it is because of His intense care about us and the world that He will not allow people to go on wrecking other people's lives or the world. That we have wrecked this world is a fact. We will not be allowed to wreck the next one. He will see that *right*, not *might*, prevails. The only way that judgment could be done away with, is for God to become quite indifferent to what is happening in His world, in fact, to become careless about everything. Such a prospect is horrific—it means that there would be no *right* or *wrong*, but that *might* would be right forever! We should thank God for the coming judgment as the Psalmist does (Psalm 98:9). That day will be full of 'righteousness and equity'. So if we love what is right, we will love everything which takes place that day. If it is not like this and there is no judgment then there is no justice ever and no ultimate difference between the wicked and the godly. It is unthinkable. God's love is not weak and sentimental. It is strong and therefore *must* issue ultimately in judgment on those who will not repent.

However there is better news to be told than that of judgment. God has intervened and there is a gospel for sinful men under judgment. God has acted for us. The nature of the gospel itself is a strong reason for telling it.

4. The nature of the gospel

What kind of gospel? Paul tells us the gospel is "the power of God for the salvation of everyone who believes: first for the Jew, then for the Gentile. For in the gospel a righteousness from God is revealed..." (Romans 1:16,17).

First the gospel is powerful. Think how powerful the gospel is! Every Christian you know became one because of the gospel. When you are at church next Sunday look around and remind yourself of its power. Look at yourself! Look what it did for you! It changed you from someone without hope, life or forgiveness into a new person, forgiven and restored into friendship with the living God. I must confess that often I am afraid to tell people the gospel because deep down I fear that nothing will happen and I will be made to appear to be a fool. Yet I have good evidence to think otherwise. It changed me! It is the God ordained way to change men and women. That is the good reason to tell it!

Second the gospel is right. God is able to treat us as if we were not sinful, although we are. He remains perfectly just and righteous Himself in doing so! How? Through the death of Jesus on our behalf, the just for the unjust. It is in the gospel that we see God's righteousness revealed. That's worth telling!

Third the gospel is good news to those who will accept it. Have you ever noticed how you want to share good news? Do you remember how the angel announced it to the shepherd? "I bring you good news of great joy...Today in the town of David a Saviour has been born to you; he is Christ the Lord" (Luke 2:10,11). The gospel is "good news of great joy" to those who are lonely, lost, unforgiven. There is a Saviour, Christ the Lord. That's certainly worth telling! To meditate on the content of the gospel will become a strong incentive to tell it to others.

5. The purpose of man

Concern for God's glory. There remains another reason why I should seek to lead my friends to Christ. Luke tells us that when Paul visited Athens, although there was everything there to captivate the tourist, he had eyes for one thing only, "...he was greatly distressed to see that the city was full of idols" (Acts 17:16). Although there was much religion, there was no worship of the true and living God. God was not honoured. He was not known, loved or obeyed. His name was not allowed there. Paul was stirred with jealousy for God's glory, as was Elijah at Mt. Carmel hundreds of years before (1 Kings 18:36,37). Paul gave it expression in preaching the gospel (Acts 17:17-20).

To pray the Lord's Prayer with meaning is to pray yourself into evangelism. As day by day you pray "Hallowed be Thy Name" ask yourself how will that prayer be answered? One way will be by men and women acknowledging Jesus as Lord. That will only take place as they hear the gospel. How distressed are you by the idolatry of Sydney, or London, or New York, or wherever you live? Distressed enough to tell them of the only One worthy of all praise? You will not keep praying that prayer with any meaning, and not become engaged in active ongoing evangelism.

Conclusion

The reasons I have given may not be exhaustive of those given in the Bible but they provide us with very strong motivation to be actively engaged in evangelism. Anyone who has the Spirit of God and who knows the Word of God as we do, knows that he should be engaged personally and actively in taking the gospel to people. We must pray that we will not harden our hearts against God's word or grieve His Holy Spirit who shows us through that word good and urgent reasons for action. To be properly motivated is to *do* and not only talk about it.

However that work is made easier by knowing that God Himself is actively engaged in that work. We need to consider the relationship between God's work and ours in the whole area of evangelism.

CHAPTER SIX

Who Does What? — God's Work and Ours

The work of evangelism is a work which God and man do together. We are called God's fellow workers when we engage in it (1 Corinthians 3:9; 2 Corinthians 6:1). However we do not do the same work. We need to be clear what is God's role, and what is our role in this work, so that we do not become confused.

God and His world

The Bible's world view is that God is Sovereign Lord and ruler over His universe. It also shows man was created with great dignity in the image of God (Genesis 1:26).*
Mankind has been given dominion over the world (Genesis 1:26) and is called upon by God to exercise authority over the creation (Psalm 8). This authority is not an independent one but is to be exercised under God's rule. In the Garden of Eden narrative we are presented with the suggestion that man can exercise his authority outside and independently of God's rule (Genesis 3:4). This is a lie. However, it continues to persist in the mind of sinful mankind. We believe ourselves independent of God. However, the Bible says differently. Paul tells us that in Jesus "all things hold together" (Colossians 1:17). Believers and unbelievers alike are dependent upon God for life. Believers and unbelievers alike exercise their

---

*It is only too easy to back up any idea with a biblical 'proof-text' taken out of context. Instead of quoting several verses I have chosen for simplicity, one which in its context illustrates the statements made. No doubt the reader will be able to recall others.

choices within the mind of God. It is impossible to be any other way. That is not to say that unbelievers recognise this fact. However, it remains a fact whether it is recognised or not.

Man, a responsible agent

God's sovereign power and rule over His creation does not obliterate man's will. God has made us responsible people. We have real wills. We make choices and are accountable to God for them. This is clearly stated by Jesus in the incident recorded in Matthew 11:20-24. Jesus had been visiting the cities Bethsaida, Capernaum and Chorazin. He had done most of His mighty works there but they did not repent. They had the best opportunity to respond. He, the finest of miracle workers and the best preacher, was there in their midst, but no one responded. This behaviour calls forth from Jesus some of the most frightening words in Scripture. "Woe to you, Chorazin! Woe to you, Bethsaida! If the miracles that were performed in you had been performed in Tyre and Sidon, they would have repented long ago in sackcloth and ashes. But I tell you, it will be more bearable for Tyre and Sidon on the day of judgment than for you" (Matthew 11:21,22). It is clear from this saying that the people are held responsible for their actions. They are to blame. Had the people of Tyre and Sidon received such a demonstration of God's Sovereign Power, they would have acted differently.

However the fact that they *are responsible* for their response does not make God less Sovereign, nor does it diminish God's control over His world any more than God's control over the world diminished mankind's responsibility for his actions.

Our real problem in trying to understand this relationship comes from the completely unique nature of it. We have real wills interacting with real wills when we encounter each other. We have no parallel of a real will interacting with a Sovereign Will. This is made doubly difficult to understand because the relationship is *described* but not explained.

The interaction between God and man is unique. It will always raise a question, 'Can God be truly God if man is truly man?'. Does not one, in some way, cancel the other? The answer is 'No'.

We have further illustrations of this unique relationship available to us which show that both can be associated together without either being diminished. In the incarnation of the Lord Jesus Christ we see both God and man. He is not less God because He is a man, any more than His humanity is restricted by His being God the Son. In the writing of Scripture we see both God and man interacting. The books were written by men and can rightly be seen to be the words of men, but they are also rightly described as the *Word of God* (Acts 4:25; Matthew 19:4; 2 Peter 1:21). They are not less the *words* of God because they are written by men, any more than the authors were reduced to 'non-persons' in the process.

God's part and man's part
Because of this relationship any action we engage in, can at any given moment, be described from God's point of view or from man's point of view (Exodus 8:15; 10:27). Sometimes it is described from both at the same time, as Paul does when he writes to the Corinthians, "I thank God, who put into the heart of Titus the same concern I have for you. For Titus not only welcomed our appeal, but he is coming to you with much enthusiasm and on his own initiative" (2 Corinthians 8:16,17).

Titus' concern for the Corinthians can be described as 'being put into his heart by God' and also as coming from 'his own initiative'. Titus does it and God is doing it.

Our coming to Christ is no different from the other ways God works in His world. He works, and we respond (Acts 13:48).

God initiates the gospel
That God and man co-operate together in evangelism is a fact, but it is God who takes the initiative. The Bible has the view that God is Sovereign Lord over the whole

creation. He is the Lord of creation (Job chapters 38 to 40), the Lord of history (Isaiah chapters 41 to 45), Lord over mankind (Acts 13:48), and the Lord of evangelism (Matthew 9:38).

This is clearly taught to us in 2 Corinthians 5:18-20. God was reconciling the world to Himself in Christ (2 Corinthians 5:19). It was the Father who sent the Son to be the Saviour of the world. It was out of His love for us that His action took place (John 3:16). It is through the work of the Son who died and rose again for us that our sins are not counted against us.

Without this work of God in Christ there could be no reconciliation between God and man. In fact there would be no gospel. God takes the initiative in providing us with the gospel. "All this is from God, who reconciled us to himself through Christ and gave us the ministry of reconciliation" (2 Corinthians 5:18).

God initiates evangelism
God also takes the initiative by calling and directing the worldwide programme of evangelism. The Bible pictures God out in front calling us to join Him in His ongoing work of evangelism and not the reverse. God took action and not only sent His Son, but as a consequence of that action commissioned the apostles and the disciples into a world wide programme of evangelism (Matthew 28:18-20; Luke 24:44-48; 2 Corinthians 5:20). Not only does God do that generally, but He directs specific acts of evangelism.

When Paul and Barnabas returned to Antioch after their first missionary journey, they gathered with the church to report about the success of this venture. Luke describes it like this, "On arriving there, they gathered the church together and reported all that God had done through them and how he had opened the door of faith to the Gentiles" (Acts 14:27). God had called and directed Paul and Barnabas to this work (Acts 13:2). God continued to work through them and it was God who 'opened a door of faith' to those who heard them.

God initiates response

Not only does God promote and direct the work of the gospel, but he initiates mankind's response to the gospel. Sinful people left to themselves are unable to turn back to God. They exercise their will by refusing to obey Him. All the adjectives used to describe sinful man demonstrate his inability to respond positively. He needs God to change him.

He is 'blind' and cannot *see* the way (2 Corinthians 4:4). He needs to have that blindness dealt with (2 Corinthians 4:6). He is 'lost' and cannot *find* the way. He needs someone to find him (Luke 19:10). He is 'dead' in spiritual matters and needs to be brought back to life (Ephesians 2:4,5). He is 'powerless' in dealing with his dilemma. He needs to be saved (Romans 5:6). He is an enemy of God and needs to be made a friend (2 Corinthians 5:20).

All these descriptions confirm the fact that sinful man cannot turn back to God and respond positively to the gospel unless God deals with him. It is not that man does not have any choice at all, he exercises his will and does exactly what he wants. Yet without God changing us we never want what we *aught*. We exercise our will by saying "no". Before a person says "yes" to God through the gospel he needs to be changed within.

This is clearly taught by Jesus in His saying, "No one can come to me unless the Father who sent me draws him, and I will raise him up at the last day" (John 6:44). This idea is consistently shown by John in his Gospel. Who is the person who has the right to become a child of God? The person who is "born not of natural descent, nor of human decision or a husband's will, but born of God" (John 1:13). It is God who brings them to birth. Who is the person who will enter the Kingdom of heaven? The person who is "born from above", or "born of the Spirit" (John 3:3,8). God does it. This truth is taught by the apostles Paul (2 Corinthians 4:1-6; Ephesians 1:3-6; Romans 8:28,29) and Peter (1 Peter 2:9; 2 Peter 1:10).

God initiates the gospel and it is He who chooses us and calls us back to Himself, changing us (John 15:16) and giving us the gift of repentance (Acts 5:31; 11:15-18) and faith (Acts 14:27; Ephesians 2:8).

It is God through His Holy Spirit, who convinces us of sin and righteousness and judgment (John 16:8-11).

It was God who opened Lydia's heart to respond to Paul's message (Acts 16:14).

It is by the work of the Holy Spirit that we are able to say "Jesus is Lord" (1 Corinthians 12:3).

It is God's work to regenerate us and give us new life (Titus 3:4-7).

He calls to Himself those He has chosen to live to His glory (Romans 8:28; Ephesians 1:11,12).

Man's part—a genuine response

The process of regeneration, which is God's work, is something of which we are usually not conscious. Sometimes we can detect that we are changing in our attitude to God, to sin, and to God's people. It is as Jesus says, like the wind. "The wind blows wherever it pleases. You hear its sound, but you cannot tell where it comes from or where it is going. So it is with everyone born of the Spirit" (John 3:8). It is like an operation performed under anaesthetic. You are more conscious of what has taken place after the operation than you are during it! The evidence that the new birth has taken place is a proper response to God and the gospel.

Before God brought me to new life I responded by exercising my will negatively. I rejected Jesus as my Lord and Saviour. I thought sin and rebellion were quite unimportant. I was careless about Christian matters. What then caused me to change and to exercise my will positively? It was God's Holy Spirit who opened my eyes and gave me the ability to repent and trust God's word. It was a real miracle.

What before seemed ridiculous and totally unimportant suddenly took on new meaning and significance. I suddenly realised that Jesus *was* Lord. He had died on the cross for *me* so that my sins would be forgiven. He really had been *raised* from the dead. I *was* in fact going to meet Him on the judgment day and what is more I was completely *unprepared* for such an eventuality. I now exercised my will in a totally different direction and said "Have mercy on me". Instead of exercising my will in rebellion and unbelief I turned back to God in repentance and faith.

The response—repentance and faith

Paul explained to the elders of the church of Ephesus that his preaching was directed towards a response of repentance and faith. "I have declared," he said "to both Jews and Greeks that they must turn to God in repentance and have faith in our Lord Jesus" (Acts 20:21).

This is the positive response which is expected from the gospel. Repentance is exercised when a person comes to terms with God as God. He recognises that he has rebelled against God and deserves God's anger. He turns from this position to one of submission. He acknowledges Jesus as his Lord and seeks to live under His authority. Repentance is more than feeling sorry, it involves a complete change of attitude towards God, and the Lord Jesus. It can be expressed in different ways. The Thessalonians are described as turning "to God from idols, to serve the living and true God" (1 Thessalonians 1:9). For Thomas a clear recognition of Jesus as "My Lord and my God" (John 20:28). For the rich young ruler it meant "Go sell everything you have and give to the poor, and you will have treasure in heaven. Then come, ˙ ʾllow me" (Mark 10:21).

When writing to the Romans Paul used the phrase "to call people...to the obedience that comes from faith" (Romans 1:5) to describe the response. Jesus in stark terms calls us to absolute surrender, "If anyone comes to me and does not hate his father and mother, his wife and children, his brothers and sisters—yes, even his own life—he cannot be my disciple. And anyone who does not carry his cross and follow me cannot be my disciple" (Luke 14:26,27). It is a 'shocking' way of saying that true repentance involves a new life style where Jesus takes precedence over family, friends and work, indeed over everything. It is another way of saying "Follow me" (Matthew 4:19).

Repentance towards God *and* faith in the Lord Jesus is the way Paul describes a correct response. The important thing about faith, in the Bible, is not so much the *act of believing* as it is the person *in whom we believe*. God the Father has declared His Son Jesus, to be Lord (Philippians 2:10). He also declares that we can be acceptable to Him because of the death of His Son (1 John 2:1,2). Jesus tells us that because of His death on our behalf we can be completely forgiven, and thus received back into fellowship with God (Matthew 20:28; 26:28; John 14:6). In fact this is the great theme of the Bible. God will send His anointed One, His Christ, into the world to save His people from their sins (Luke 2:32; 2:11; Matthew 1:21). It is through the death and resurrection of Jesus that we can be cleansed from all sin (1 John 1:7). So to exercise faith in the Lord Jesus is to believe that He *is* who He is and to believe that He has *done* what He has done. That is, I believe what God says about Jesus. I believe that He will forgive me and will accept me, not because I am good, not because I try hard, not because I did the best I could but because of Jesus and His work on my behalf.

The answer to the question, "If God were to say to you, 'Is there any reason why I should let you into heaven?'" will show clearly where a person's faith is pinned. The Christian would answer "Because Jesus Christ has died for me".

Not one without the other

From time to time I meet people who seem to be trying to make a part response to the gospel. They seem to have exercised faith in Jesus for the forgiveness of sins. They appear to trust Jesus as their Saviour but there has been no accompanying change in behaviour, no real repentance. The idea that God should rule their lives is completely foreign to them. There has been no real regeneration, although there has been a genuine desire to 'go to heaven', or to seek relief from a guilty conscience. Such people wish the benefit of the death of Jesus without the accompanying fellowship with Jesus. They wish to relate to Jesus as if He was not King in God's world. There can be no faith in the Lord Jesus without repentance towards God.

On the other hand, there are those who effect a real reformation in life thinking that such a change is repentance, but who never trust the Lord Jesus for forgiveness. They genuinely seek to obey God and live under His authority, and believe that by doing so they will earn God's approval. This error also shows that there has been no genuine regeneration. They have not truly repented. There can be no repentance towards God without faith in the Lord Jesus Christ. Such an attitude would render the death of the Lord Jesus quite unnecessary.

'How' is not 'that'

Much stress has already been laid on God's work in sending Jesus, directing evangelism, calling men and women, and giving them His Holy Spirit to regenerate them. We may well ask, "What is the role of the one who shares the gospel?". The truth is that God does in fact, do this work through us (2 Corinthians 5:20). We are fellow workers with God (1 Corinthians 3:9; 2 Corinthians 6:1). *That* God calls men and women to Himself is a fact. *How* God does it is through our preaching of the gospel and our prayers. These are the God ordained ways through which He normally works and through which He has promised to work (Romans 10:17; Colossians 4:3,4). He does not usually do so independently of these means. It is through the "folly of what we preach" that God "saves those who believe" (1 Corinthians 1:21). Paul says "I am not ashamed of the gospel, because it is the power of God for the salvation of everyone who believes" (Romans 1:16). He knows that as he preaches the gospel God will use it to convince the hearer of its truth (2 Corinthians 4:5,6) and will enable that person to respond in repentance and faith.

Some people have expressed the idea that preaching is a waste of time unless God has regenerated the hearer, as if God did His work apart from His Word. No indeed! It is through His Word that He works (Genesis 1:3). How does He bring us to faith? The apostle Paul explains that "faith comes from hearing the message, and the message is heard through the word of Christ" (Romans 10:17). Consequently we are not to be inactive, but eager to tell people the gospel. It is the powerful way God saves people.

When we meet people who say they would like to believe but they genuinely cannot, we should encourage them to ask God to give them faith since it is a gift. But since we know that faith comes by hearing the Word of God, we should encourage them to read the Gospels and to come and hear the gospel preached. The genuine measure of wanting to believe can be gauged by whether a person will listen to the gospel.

In addition to preaching, God has also created prayer as the means whereby He works in the lives of men and women. James reminds us of the effectiveness of it (James 4:16). This is so in evangelism as well as in every other area of life. Paul urges the Colossians to "pray for us that God may open to us a door for the word, to declare the mystery of Christ...that I may make it clear as I ought to speak" (Colossians 4:3,4). Since evangelism is a spiritual activity, it must be approached spiritually. It is never a matter of learning a technique nor is it just a matter of preaching the gospel; prayer should be made that God will open the 'eyes' of the hearer's understanding (2 Corinthians 4:6) and that God will grant them repentance and faith.

Faithfulness is what matters

To see both God's work and ours in proper perspective should relieve us of the pressure to 'get results' in terms of the number of people who are converted, and as such should free us to get on and do the work of evangelism more and more. Our effectiveness must never be gauged on how many people respond, but on our faithfulness to the gospel and in telling it. We should rejoice when many are converted and be sad when many are not. But remember, that the response is not in our hands. Faithfulness in preaching the gospel, and in prayer is what God is looking for (1 Corinthians 4:2).

It is the fact that we do not have to manufacture results or manipulate people to get them which caused Paul to say, "We have renounced secret and shameful ways; we do not use deception, nor do we distort the word of God. On the contrary, by setting forth the truth plainly we commend ourselves to every man's conscience in the sight of God" (2 Corinthians 4:2). He was not unaware of the problem confronting him. He knew that "The god of this age has blinded the minds of unbelievers, so that they cannot see the light of the gospel of the glory of Christ, who is the image of God" (2 Corinthians 4:4). However, he was not deterred because his role was clear. "For we do not preach ourselves, but Jesus Christ as Lord, and ourselves as your servants for Jesus' sake" (2 Corinthians 4:5). Reponse is in the hands of God (2 Corinthians 4:6).

Jesus, the perfect example

The incident in the life of Jesus already referred to is helpful in our understanding of how God's work and ours interact in the area of evangelism.

Matthew, in his Gospel, tells us that Jesus had been working in the cities of Chorazin, Bethsaida and Capernaum. This work of teaching and of performing miracles, although great, met with no response of repentance. In their midst was the best of communicators and the finest miracle worker, yet there was no positive response (Matthew 11:20). Whose fault was it? Jesus held them responsible for their actions. "Woe unto you," He said to them all. He explained that others would have responded differently had they had such an opportunity, and because of this the judgment of God on the people of these three cities would be greater (Matthew 11:21-24). They were held responsible for their actions.

There is no doubt that such a 'fruitless' mission must have caused deep distress to Jesus. He was sustained however, by the fact that God is sovereign in His work of evangelism and results are in His hand. He prayed "I praise you, Father, Lord of heaven and earth, because you have hidden these things from the wise and learned, and revealed them to little children. Yes, Father, for this was your good pleasure" (Matthew 11:25,26). However, this knowledge did not deter Him from pressing on with preaching the gospel "Come to me, all you who are weary and burdened, and I will give you rest" (Matthew 11:28).

People have suggested that this view of God's sovereignty in evangelism will lead to laziness and lack of real zeal on our part. It did not in the case of Jesus (Matthew 11:28). It did not in the case of Paul (2 Corinthians 4:5). If it does in ours, it must be because we have not rightly understood it. It should have the opposite effect.

The fact that God is sovereign in the work of evangelism and that it is He who calls out the elect, raises the question, "Why doesn't God choose everyone?" That is the subject of the next chapter.

CHAPTER SEVEN

Why Doesn't God Choose Everyone?

Salvation is a work which God does, and man's positive response to the gospel depends on it (John 6:35-44). God loves the world (John 3:16) and does not wish any one to perish (2 Peter 3:9). Given this then, why doesn't God choose everyone? Why is there an apparent contradiction between God's character and God's unfolding plan for the world?

An unexplained mystery
The Bible opens up with a world created by God where everything is good (Genesis 1:31). Man is at peace with himself, with his fellow man, with his environment and most of all with God. In this world we are confronted, without any explanation, with the serpent (Genesis 3:1). He is crafty and above all he is against God and everything God stands for. He aims to destroy man (Genesis 3:4,5) and he works to that end.

It is here that we have the unexplained mystery. Why did God allow into His plan that which is obviously against His character? We are quickly introduced to a warfare which is bigger and more significant than a fight between man and God. Before man rebels against God the battle lines are drawn up. There is warfare in the spirit world (Revelation 12:7) and man is persuaded to join the wrong side. God calls on us to change sides (Acts 17:30; Matthew 3:2) so that we will not be destroyed when He deals with Satan and all the enemies of God (2 Thessalonians 2:8).

We do not know *why* God allowed this to take place

but we do know *that* He allowed it. It happened within the area of His control. It didn't overtake Him and catch Him 'on the hop'. However, once it is allowed we are plunged into the problem. Why does God appear to do (His plan) what is unlike Himself (His character)? The Bible does not resolve this problem, consequently we cannot know the reason. However, since the apparent contradiction is not given a biblical solution we must take care not to try and solve the problem by minimising either of the truths. Some people do this by suggesting that God has limited His control, His sovereignty, or by suggesting that man does not really have a will of his own. Either view is without evidence in the Bible. We are to hold both truths in tension as the Bible does.

God uses good and evil

Why God allowed sin and evil into the creation we are not told, but it is clear that everything remains under God's control. This can be clearly seen in the fact that God uses both repentant people and good events and sinful people and unhappy events, to bring His plans to completion. He also sets conditions on the abilities of Satan (Job 1:12; 2:6).

Sin is not less sinful because it is used by God to fulfil His ultimate purposes. Nor does it excuse the person who does the action as if he was not responsible. This is clearly demonstrated in the life of Joseph (Genesis chapters 37 to 50), and in the events surrounding the death of the Lord Jesus (Acts 2:22-24).

The life of Joseph

Everything surrounding the early part of this story is a long succession of sinful and unjust dealings. Joseph was a favourite (Genesis 37:3,4). He was hated by his brothers because of this. Their jealousy was fanned into flames by Joseph relating to them his dream, which although not calculated to 'win friends and influence people', nevertheless should not have caused the reaction it did (Genesis 37:8-11). When opportunity arose they decided to murder him. This action was only averted by the persuasive tongue of Reuben who proposed to save him when the brothers come to be of better mind. However, while Reuben was away they sold Joseph to a group of Midianite slave traders and then lied to their father about his fate. No one can doubt that this young man was much sinned against! Jealousy, murder, treachery, lying, all make up the list of sins against this man.

Joseph was sold in Egypt into the household of Potiphar where eventually he became overseer (Genesis 39:1-6). But his troubles were not over. Potiphar's wife called on him to enter into an adulterous relationship with her and when he refused, she accused him of rape and he was cast into prison (Genesis 39:9-23). Here his life took a new turn, and although he again suffered through the sinful forgetfulness of Pharoah's butler (Genesis 40:23), in time he was promoted to a position of great authority in Egypt (Genesis 45:5). When his brothers came to Egypt to buy grain he had a golden opportunity to even an old score with them! He did not harm them because he realised that although they "had meant to do evil against him, God had meant it for good" (Genesis 50:2). They were not excused for their actions as if sin was not sin. "You meant it for evil against me," said Joseph. Still, God uses both good and evil in bringing His plan to completion.

It was not as if God made the best of a developing crisis. He knew from the beginning what would happen. This is witnessed to by Joseph's dream (Genesis 37:5-9). The brothers acted in exactly the way they wanted to, and were consequently responsible for their sins. They were acting in a way which is contrary to God's character, yet all the time it was within the framework of God's plan. He used them as part of His ultimate plan to bring good to pass. He is completely Sovereign. Some actions which are opposed to God's character are allowed in the developing plan. It *is* a mystery without explanation.

The death of Jesus

The New Testament has a parallel illustration of this truth. It is the death of Jesus. Everything surrounding

Jesus' death speaks of treachery, greed, sin, weakness and corruption. The betrayal of Judas for money (Luke 22:1-5); the unorthodox procedures of the Council (John 11:45-49); the weakness of Pilate (Luke 23:22-25); the carelessness of the people (Luke 23:13-23); are all sinful actions.

Peter explains in his sermon on the day of Pentecost, that it all happened according to the "definite plan and foreknowledge of God" (Acts 2:23). They were not puppets acting by some string-pulling deity. They were plain, ordinary, sinful men and women running 'true to form'. Judas was a thief (John 12:6) and as such, happy to betray Jesus for money (Luke 22:5). He was responsible for his actions. The Council were political schemers, the mob oscillated as ever. Pilate was a peace-at-any-price governor. They did as they liked and were responsible for the way they acted. Their actions were against the character of God but not outside of His plan or control.

God's character and His plan

Because of the above truth the term 'the will of God' is ambiguous. Sometimes it is used in the Bible to mean "God's plan" (Ephesians 1:11) and sometimes it is used to describe "God's character" (2 Peter 3:9). A simple illustration will show what I mean. See how difficult it is to answer the question, "Was it God's will for Judas to betray Jesus?". You want to answer both "Yes" and "No". However the ambiguity disappears when I ask, "Was it a God-like action for Judas to betray Jesus?". Answer, "No!" Or again, "Was it in God's plan for Judas to betray Jesus?". Answer, "Yes." Now when we come to verses where the term 'the will of God' is used we will have to determine from the context whether the verse is speaking about God's character, which is sinless, or God's plan, where both good and evil may be used. I understand the verses in 2 Peter 3:8-10 to be referring to God's character. He is a God who does not wish any person to perish, but all to reach repentance. If we ask the question, "Is this God's plan?" the answer appears to be different (Matthew 6:13,14).

The Christian person is assured that God will bring His plan to pass (Ephesians 1:9,10). We neither know when or how God will do it. This is not our business; we are called on to be men and women who reflect God's character (Genesis 1:26) and as we do that we will be used by the Sovereign God to live to His glory.

It is possible to discriminate and act rightly

It is a mystery to us as to why God doesn't choose everyone. It seems baffling to us. We cannot solve it because it is an extension of the wider problem of evil in God's good world. To describe a problem is not to solve it. Since the Bible doesn't solve it, we cannot—at least not with any certainty. There are some parallels in life which can help us to be happier living in such a paradox.

We are aware in life's situations choices are made between people, and that such choices can be correct. An example can be seen in the selection of a cricket team to represent the country. Only eleven players can play, so from all the hundreds of players a selection has to be made. We recognise the rightness of making a selection and (sometimes!) we agree with the actual selection because we know the basis of the selection. We do not hesitate to say '*A* has been rightly chosen and *B* has been rightly excluded'. On the other hand, imagine you are in court one day and a judge passes two different sentences on two men for apparently identical crimes. He sends one to prison and the other he allows out on bail. Again I am able to approve this discrimination when I know the background circumstances and the previous criminal records of both parties.

Now when we come to God's elective purpose we know that God will act rightly because He is righteous and holy. He loves justice and hates what is unfair. He is loving and merciful. We know it *is* possible to select and act rightly and we know that God's selection springs from His mercy. Our problem in understanding comes because we do not know the total basis on which the selection is made. We know that it isn't on the basis of goodness or anything in us (Romans 9:9-13) since all people are sinful (Romans 3:12), but we must not conclude that to make a choice is wrong, simply because *we* cannot work out the basis on which it is made. God's mercy is sovereign (Romans 9:19-24) and both it and God's love are basic in the doctrine of election.

Once again it is important to note that to describe a life parallel is not to solve the mystery. The mystery remains because God has not chosen to tell us the basis on which selection is made. We must not resolve the problem by affirming on the basis of 2 Peter 3:8,9 that all people will be saved, or on the basis of Matthew 6:13,14 or similar verses that man can thwart the plan of God. To be godly is to receive the word of God and live within the confines of it.

How should we react?

What effect should this have on our evangelism? It should cause us to be like God and long that all people will be saved. We should pray that God will open the 'eyes' of those we speak to. We should be eager to preach the gospel to people because we know this is the way God calls people to Himself. We should trust God when we are confronted with this mystery and not attribute wrong motives to Him. The prophet Habakkuk, confronted with the same problem, could not find an answer but knew that the godly person lived by trusting God (Habakkuk 2:4). He reminded himself that God is a faithful and trustworthy God and so he continued to trust God (Habakkuk 3:26-29), although he didn't seem to get an answer to his question (Habakkuk 1:12-17).

God does not exercise His sovereign will by ignoring our will. He does not mock us when He calls on "all men everywhere to repent" (Acts 27:30).

We may not know why God does not choose everyone for His special mercy but we know exactly what *we* should do. We should both pray and work so that the gospel will be taken to everyone (Matthew 28:16).

The next question to be looked at is "What is the responsibility of ordained ministers to their congregations in the work of evangelism?".

CHAPTER EIGHT

The Minister, the Church and Evangelism

So far I have set out to show that every Christian is to be actively involved in evangelism by life style and by word of mouth. I want to show that the minister in his role as pastor/teacher of the congregation is to train the Christians for their work in gospelling. Basically evangelism is not a congregational activity, but an individual one. The congregation as it gathers will offer help and support, and will encourage as well as train the individual (1 Corinthians 14). If this is not the case the individual will find his role in evangelism so hard he probably will not continue at it for very long.

Evangelism—a way of life
It is the privilege as well as the responsibility of every Christian to be engaged in evangelism. The way in which that involvement manifests itself will vary from person to person according to each one's gifts and opportunities. A person who is in hospital and attended by Christian nursing staff, will have limited opportunity with unbelievers, whereas others, like Billy Graham, can tell the gospel to millions. In any case whatever the opportunities and however varied our gifts, our ultimate aim is that evangelism will become a way of life. Any and every situation is one in which we *are to witness, by the way we live*, to the fact that Jesus is our Lord.

Equally, any and every situation is one where we may *be able to witness, by speaking*, of that same Lord. Any situation in which we find ourselves in relationship with others is a potential evangelistic situation.

The Christian—the unit for evangelism
We have seen that every Christian is to live with
gospelling in mind (1 Corinthians Chapters 8 to 11:1). He
is to be ready and able to give an answer to anyone who
asks him to give a reason for the "hope that he has" (1
Peter 3:15). He is to be able to do this for anyone at any
time. He cannot be sure that he will be called upon to do
this only when other Christians are present, and
consequently he is to be self-sufficient as an evangelising
unit. He cannot rely on the others to do his work in this
regard.

Evangelistic initiative is *personal*—it is not primarily a
congregational activity, although the congregation (the
church) has a vital part to play in encouraging and
equipping each Christian in his work. Christians may
decide to join with other Christians to help in their
evangelism, as in two Christians doing door-to-door
visiting or uniting with all the members in the
congregation at an evangelistic service or rally.

These collective activities ought not to be allowed to
move the responsibility from 'me' to 'us' which too easily
degenerates into 'them'. Nor should the individual
Christians wait until their church organises them into
some area of evangelism. We are to encourage each other
to be praying and looking for opportunities to tell people
the gospel. However, I do not want to suggest that the
congregation plays no part in this, nor do I wish to
depreciate its importance nor the absolute necessity for
Christians to meet with the church. The Bible knows
nothing of isolated believers. Both the minister and the
congregation have a crucial part to play.

Prepare God's people for service   .
Paul, in the Epistle to the Ephesians, makes an
impassioned plea for the congregation to be united
together. He gives us a very impressive list of reasons why
we should work hard to maintain the unity among the
believers (Ephesians 4:1-6), for it is in the company of
these people that together we will grow up with Christ

(Ephesians 4:13-15). This will be done through each Christian exercising his or her gifts in the congregation. Those gifts are given through the graciousness of the ascended Christ. However, some gifts are so important that unless they are used publicly, the rest of us do not know how to exercise similarly the gifts which we have been given.

Paul tells us "It was he (Jesus) who gave some to be apostles, some to be prophets, some to be evangelists, and some to be pastors and teachers, to prepare God's people for works of service, so that the body of Christ may be built up..." (Ephesians 4:11-12). This is not the place to enter into a discussion on whether the gifts of apostles and prophets were for the early church in order to establish it until the scriptures were available, or whether they still exist today. However, it is important to notice two facts.

1. All these gifts were 'word' gifts. In one way or another they all brought God's word to the other members of the congregation whether they were apostles, prophets, evangelists or pastors.

2. These 'word' gifts were crucial for the other members to know how to exercise their own gifts. They prepared God's people for works of service.

It may not be easy to identify all these gifts now, but at least the pastor/teachers can be identified. There is no doubt that that gift is still with us. It is through the proper and careful teaching of the Bible by the pastor/teacher, that the congregation will learn how to exercise their gifts. Nothing is more pathetic in a congregation where the 'word' gifts are neglected, than to see the inevitably tragic results of many dedicated members exercising their gifts in misguided and mis-taken ways and directing their efforts towards false and inadequate goals. Nothing is more exciting to see than a faithful and careful ministry of the 'word' gifts, one which has produced a good and clear function and direction of the congregation's gifts. That congregation grows into the 'whole measure of the fulness of Christ'. The pastor/teacher is a lynchpin in this programme.

The minister as an evangelist?

When Paul the Apostle wrote to the young man Timothy, whom he had sent to minister in the church of Ephesus, he urged him to take his preaching seriously. The exhortation he was given is one of the strongest in the Bible. "In the presence of God and of Christ Jesus, who will judge the living and the dead, and in view of his appearing and his kingdom, I give you this charge: Preach the Word; be prepared in season and out of season; correct, rebuke and · encourage—with great patience and careful instruction" (2 Timothy 4:1,2). Paul continued in this context to urge Timothy, who we know was timid by temperament, (1 Timothy 4:12; 2 Timothy 1:7,8), do "do the work of an evangelist, discharge all the duties of your ministry" (2 Timothy 4:5).

Why did Paul need to urge him to do the work of an evangelist? Was it because Timothy was reticent and thought he may not have the gifts? If so, then Timothy's excuses were quickly dealt with! He is to do the work of an evangelist *because* he is a teacher of God's word. As a teacher he must be able to teach the evangel, and so it is proper to urge him to do so.

For too long we have driven a wedge between teaching as a function and preaching the gospel or evangelising. Paul describes the way the Christians were converted in Colossae in these terms "...you have already heard about in the word of truth, the gospel that has come to you. All over the world this gospel is producing fruit and growing, just as it has been doing among you since the day you heard it and understood God's grace in all its truth. You learned it from Epaphras" (Colossians 1:5-7).

Notice the words used to describe what happened. They *heard*, *understood* and *learned* the gospel. Epaphras taught it to them. He was the teacher/evangelist. The gospel cannot be *caught* unless it is *taught*. Timothy is urged to do the same. He is urged to "do the work of an evangelist, discharge all the duties of your ministry" (2 Timothy 4:5), because that was part of "preaching the word" (2 Timothy 4:1,2).

Today we have to be reminded afresh that ministers because of their teaching office, need to "do the work of an evangelist" as well as take responsibility to teach the congregation not only to articulate the gospel but the necessary techniques with which to do so. This will be done through special courses and through the minister's own evangelistic preaching on a regular, though not necessarily 'every service' basis.

There is a problem with churches who have evangelistic services every Sunday. It seems that they can easily degenerate into a constant call on the 'converted' to be converted, of course thus leaving those who regularly attend that service woefully uninstructed in the overall content of the Bible. Most members of a congregation cannot bring their unconverted friends every Sunday, and so tend not to ask them at all. There is a similar problem with churches where there is never an evangelistic message preached at a Sunday service.

Evangelistic services held from time to time not only give members a special function to which they can invite their friends, but they themselves can hear their minister evangelising through his preaching. They hear and in time, learn how to articulate the gospel themselves. This is a very important part of equipping God's people for their work of ministry. Not only will they learn the content of the gospel from this source, but they will also be made aware of the urgency to call men and women to repent.

A pulpit ministry which teaches the necessity of evangelism but never does it, or which stresses the urgency of the call of the gospel but never practises it, in the end cannot be sustained. Evangelistic preaching will, like the New Testament, be varied. It is impossible to reduce the New Testament to a simple form and cover its multitude of aspects. That is why the New Testament is the way it is, and like a diamond which flashes light in every direction, the gospel in its many facets is never monotonous.

Some evangelistic preaching can be monotonous because the preacher will not discipline himself to preach the gospel from the *many* New Testament statements of it, and so the sermon is always predictable. Evangelistic preaching may sometimes focus on some aspect of apologetics as well as the gospel. This also will be a valuable teaching experience for the Christians who will learn how to answer their friends. Generally speaking, this will not give most Christians sufficient training in that area but it should stimulate their thinking, reading and whet their appetites for a basic training programme in apologetics.

The minister—a playing coach

As well as teaching the members of the congregation the gospel, the minister will by way of example show members how to evangelise. Although ministers may not like it, and may wish it was otherwise, there is no doubt that most members of the congregation grow in the Christian life to be like them.

More than any other member, the minister is exposed to the congregation. When he stops reading the Bible, they tend to! When he stops saying his prayers, they tend to! When he gossips, they tend to! Conversely when he reads the Bible, says his prayers, loves the brethren, they also tend to follow. This holds good for evangelism. When he retreats into the seclusion of his study and the exclusive company of church people, other members of the congregation tend to follow the example and retreat into a 'religious' world instead of being in the real world.

I am not sure why this happens but I have observed it again and again. I think it is because when as a minister I stop reading the Bible and praying, I forget to remind others to do it, privately or in my sermons. The minister can never urge people, with any conviction, to do what he himself does not, or will not, do. However, when the minister is actively engaged in evangelism, he will know both the thrill of the challenge, and the real difficulties involved, and consequently will teach his people to evangelise others with zeal and sympathy. The person who teaches must be actively involved in the activity.

Several years ago I visited some churches in the U.S.A. who were actively engaged in evangelism and two in particular illustrate what I have been saying.

In church *A* I questioned the minister—"Do you think every member in the congregation should be active in evangelism?"

"No! Only those who have the gifts. You can trust the Holy Spirit to raise up those with such gifts."

"Do you give any special training to those with the gifts for evangelism?"

"No! Apart from the teaching from the pulpit which everyone gets."

In church *B* the same questions.

"Do you think every member should be active in evangelism?"

"Yes! All Christians are under obligation to seek opportunities to tell the gospel whenever that is possible."

"Do you give them special training?"

"Yes! How can you expect people to do the work if they are not trained. We run courses in every method we know."

In basic outlook the ministers in churches A and B could not have been different, yet my observation of the attitude to evangelism of the church members of both congregations seemed identical. Both congregations were committed to the work. Both congregations gave it a high priority. Both congregations were actively engaged in the work. Both congregations were seeing a steady stream of converts. What had caused this? It was the *practice* of the ministers. They were both actively engaged in regular ongoing programmes to get the gospel out to the people. Both were skilful in doing this and in spite of their differences in outlook, both had produced the same results in the congregation by example!

The minister—a trainer

Evangelism Explosion, Campus Crusade and *The Navigators* have all shown the value of 'on the spot' training. If the minister is to equip God's people for the work of ministry he will need to give special training to His people.

These training programmes need to include:

(a) *Growth in godliness*
(b) *A clear gospel presentation in a form which is easy to reproduce*

(c) *Time to practise that gospel presentation*

(d) *Training in the technique to be adopted when using that particular presentation*

(e) *Formation of an ongoing fellowship/nurture group to encourage and help members*

Since Christians are different and have different abilities they won't all be able to use a given technique. Each individual Christian is to be helped to find a way in which he can give expression to the gospel. Some will be able to use their home for evangelism, others will do door-to-door visiting. Some will visit hospitals and teach in schools, others will visit 'shut-ins'.

Offering variety in training will not only help each Christian individually, but will relieve some of the guilt feeling which accompanies 'failure' of those members who are unable to use any one particular technique. I consider if I push a Christian to use a technique which he cannot master then *I* have failed, not *he*. Nothing causes Christians to withdraw from evangelism more than the guilt riddled conscience which comes from repeated failure. Nothing causes Christians to be zealous in evangelism than finding them a way in which they can work with confidence within the framework of their gifts. This means that some selection needs to be made when offering training, and probably people should be invited individually to train rather than a course be offered widely to the congregation. It is obvious that when such a smorgasbord of methods is available, they cannot all be offered simultaneously.

It may be that a wide variety of training may not be within the scope or ability of the minister. He needs to bring in other specialists to train his people in areas in which he has no knowledge or real gifts himself. He is not, nor should he be expected to be, 'omni-competent' in all methods but he should take responsibility to see that individuals are cared for and trained.

The congregation—a support

As more and more members in the congregation begin to engage in evangelism, then there will be a need for real supportive fellowship within the congregation. This work is always difficult. We all need to be reminded that 'failure is not final'. We all need to be reminded of the value and importance of this work. We all need the encouragement to continue working at it. This should come from within the fellowship of the congregation.

It will probably be essential in large congregations for people engaged in evangelism to be encouraged to join in some supportive groups where they can be prayed for and encouraged.

Conclusion

The work of evangelism is personal. Each individual Christian has a responsibility to engage in evangelistic work. The individual Christian is the basic unit for evangelism. He may join with other Christians for efficiency of work in evangelism. Both minister and congregation have an important part to play in the equipment and ongoing encouragement of the individual. Why is it always so hard to do the work of evangelism?

CHAPTER NINE

Why is Evangelism Always so Hard?

For many years I was not able to admit to anyone how really difficult I found it to try to speak to people about Jesus. I thought there must be something wrong with me and sometimes I even doubted whether I was a Christian because of this fear. This spark of a doubt would flare up into a flame whenever I was challenged with a question like, "How many people have you led to Christ?"

It was a long time before I discovered that almost all Christians were like I was—some even more so! All Christians are tempted to be ashamed of the gospel. If there were no such temptations then we would never have been warned by Jesus with such a strong warning, "If anyone is ashamed of me and my words in this adulterous and sinful generation, the Son of Man will be ashamed of him when he comes in his Father's glory with the holy angels" (Mark 8:38). Neither would Paul have needed to sound such a strong warning to Timothy "So do not be ashamed to testify about our Lord, or ashamed of me his prisoner: but join with me in suffering for the gospel by the power of God, who has saved us and called us to a holy life..." (2 Timothy 1:8,9).

Many people believe that the presence of such temptation shows that they don't really have any gifts for evangelism, and use it to opt out. Neither Jesus nor Paul would allow us to think that way. Like all temptations it is to be resisted. These are good reasons why we should not be ashamed. Nevertheless the temptation is real and should be recognised and dealt with. I have come to see that the 'great' ones in the Bible faced temptations as we do. This has been a help to me. We are always under pressure to be ashamed of the gospel and the Bible tells us how to resist such temptation.

The gospel is divisive

There are good reasons why we are tempted. The gospel is divisive. Jesus said, "Do not suppose that I have come to bring peace to the earth. I did not come to bring peace, but a sword. For I have come to turn 'a man against his father, a daughter against her mother, a daughter-in-law against her mother-in-law. A man's enemies will be the members of his own household" (Matthew 10:34-36). Many Christians have known only too well the adverse reaction to their own conversion by friends and relatives. Neither the gospel nor the gospel-bringer has been welcomed!

The gospel appears weak and foolish

Paul reminds us that the "message of the cross is foolishness to those who are perishing, but to us who are being saved it is the power of God" (1 Corinthians 1:18).

There is a large gap here. On the one hand we find it hard to understand why people cannot see the wonder of the gospel, while they for their part think the whole 'deal' is folly. Consequently they will think we who bring them the gospel are fools also. The apostle further spells this out—"we preach Christ crucified: a stumbling block to Jews and foolishness to Gentiles" (1 Corinthians 1:23). To the Jews, the religiously unconverted, the gospel is a terrible offence because it says your religious observances and your good life are all so much rubbish. They really stand in the way of your coming back to God. No wonder they think the gospel (and the gospeller) foolish. To the Greeks, the intellectual sophisticates, it is nonsense—so simple—so humiliating to be told that man left to himself cannot even stumble onto the truth about God, let alone make himself right with God. Because of this we will be under pressure to try and make the gospel sound 'better' and more palatable. We will be tempted to be ashamed of it. From an ordinary point of view the gospel

will always appear feeble and unimpressive, and any one
of the following often helps this view:

(a) *The incarnation*
(b) *A dying God?*
(c) *The church*

(a) *The incarnation:* If we had been in Bethlehem when
Jesus was born we would have been totally unimpressed
by the event. We would not have looked in the stinking
stable for the Lord of Glory any more than the average
man did! Who would have suspected that a momentous
event—the momentous event of all the ages, was taking
place? The Word made flesh was dwelling among us full
of grace and truth (John 1:14) and who recognised it? No
one except a handful of shepherds! They wouldn't have
recognised it either except for a brilliant revelation from
God (Luke 2:8-12). The rest of the world was oblivious to
the event. Only the eye of faith will see it for what it is.
The unbeliever will be unimpressed.

This is illustrated in that wonderful painting of
Bruegel titled "The Numbering at Bethlehem". Like all
his works the canvas is full of people. In one corner there
is a frozen pond on which children are playing. A man is
fishing in a hole. In the background a house is being
erected. There is a long queue of people lined up to be
enrolled and to pay their taxes. People are tending their
pigs, chickens and hens feed in the foreground. Life goes
on in a flurry of activity, no one takes any notice of the
figure on the donkey or the man with her. Indeed you are
hardly conscious of Mary and Joseph, the carpenter. Only
a tell-tale saw over his shoulder gives him away. You
have to search for them in the crowd. No one is taking
any notice of them. Unless you are 'in the know' and
unless you search you won't find them. They are not
really impressive. It is brilliant and absolutely accurate in
the impression it makes.

We however, in an effort to make it impressive put the
event into a 'make-believe' *un*reality. The stable is
cleaned up! The animals are all interested and jolly and
glad. There is a glow around it all; and Christmas is
made to seem anything except the tragedy which caused

the Son of God to become poor so that we might become rich.

(b) A dying God? The servant-God seems so impossible! James and John met that problem. Matthew records in his Gospel how their mother asked Jesus, "Grant that one of these two sons of mine may sit at your right and the other at your left in your kindgom" (Matthew 20:21). With eyes only for status and power, she is in effect asking that in the new cabinet her sons may have the portfolios of treasurer and minister for foreign affairs!! No wonder the others are indignant (Matthew 20:24)—they all wanted the best places themselves.

Jesus begins to tell them that the Kingdom, which is the gospel, works on the reverse principle to the world, "The Son of Man did not come to be served, but to serve, and to give his life a ransom for many" (Matthew 20:28). No wonder it appears unimpressive! No wonder we are tempted to be ashamed.

Peter had the same problem when at Caesarea Philippi Jesus told them of His forthcoming death. Prior to that, Peter in a moment of wonderful revelation, had declared his belief that Jesus is "the Christ, the Son of the living God" (Matthew 16:16). For that he received high praise from Jesus. However, when Jesus began to spell out the nature of the work of the Christ in terms of death and resurrection, it seemed so impossible to believe. Peter remonstrated, "This shall never happen to you!" Jesus' answer to him is salutary to us as well. "Out of my sight, Satan! You are a stumbling block to me; you do not have in mind the things of God, but the things of men" (Matthew 16:22,23).

How feeble the death of Jesus seems. It is about weakness and defeat. No wonder people think the preaching of the cross is folly! Again only the eye of faith can see that the death of Jesus in sin-bearing is actually the defeat of Satan (Colossians 2:15). What a brilliant moment of revelation is given to the dying thief crucified at the same time as Jesus! "Jesus," he said "remember me when you come into your kingdom" (Luke 23:42). Did ever Jesus look less like a king? Certainly not at the cleansing of the temple, or at the raising of Lazarus, when walking on the water or healing the man born blind. But there on the cross He looked weak and feeble. No wonder the other thief taunted Him as did the rulers, "Aren't you the Christ? Save yourself and us!" (Luke 23:39). Even Pilate's notice "This is the King of the Jews" was in mocking scorn.

Yet for all that, this was the moment of His glory. He was truly entering into His kingly power. Would James and John have pressed their request had they understood what it meant to be on His right hand and His left when He entered His Kingdom? I doubt it. The dying thief saw the gospel. He recognised Jesus as God's appointed King. He confessed Jesus as Lord and asked Him for mercy. It is clear that he demonstrated repentance and faith and he was rewarded with the promise of eternal life. "I tell you the truth, today you will be with me in paradise" (Luke 23:43). So unimpressive was the outward appearance that even the disciples ran away and forsook Jesus (Mark 14:50,51). No wonder we are tempted to be ashamed of the gospel! No wonder it is a stumbling block to the Jews and folly to the Greeks. Only faith will cause us to see it as it is. It is the power of God to save (Romans 1:16).

(c) *The church.* Who would believe that your local church, the one that meets at St. Oggs on Sunday at 9.30 a.m., with Mr & Mrs Bloggs and their two fidgeting boys, old Mr Snooks and the other half-dozen people, is actually going to make known God's wisdom "to the rulers and authorities in the heavenly realms" (Ephesians 3:10)? Only the eye of faith will see that! But if it doesn't, we will always have itchy feet as we endlessly search for the pure church which we believe will impress the world. It is hard to come to terms with this.

I have often noticed that when people invite Christians to give a testimony at evangelistic rallies they often choose a 'great one' in the world's eyes, either a sportsman or an actress, a pop star and even sometimes a politician. Why is this? Is it because they are not typical and not the general ordinary run-of-the-mill Christian (1 Corinthians 1:26-31)? The church which is called into being by the gospel bears the marks of the gospel. No wonder we are tempted to be ashamed of the gospel! We will need good reasons to resist that temptation.

Opposition is irrational
On the last night Jesus had with the apostles before His death He warned them of the opposition they would encounter simply because they belonged to Him. "If the world hates you, keep in mind that it hated me first...If they persecuted me, they will persecute you also...Now they have seen these miracles, and yet they have hated both me and my Father. But this is to fulfil what is written in their Law: 'They hated me without reason'" (John 15:18,20,24,25). The Jews had every reason to believe in Jesus and recognise Him to be the Messiah. He fulfilled the teaching of the Old Testament prophets. His signs were so impressive that the authorities sought to get rid of the evidence (John 12:9). Everything He did was directed towards the welfare of people, yet they hated without a cause. Opposition to Jesus was *irrational*. Opposition to Jesus' disciples will be the same.

Many have known what it is to be ostracised for no other reason than that they belong to Jesus. Many have known that where they work it is usual for Buddhists or Moslems to be treated as normal people, but all hell has broken loose when a man says "I belong to Christ". I am not referring to that proper, rational and thoroughly understandable opposition to those particular Christians who make themselves nuisances by not doing their work and embarrassing everyone by their insensitive behaviour. *They* get what they deserve and make it difficult for the rest. I am speaking about that opposition which comes simply because one belongs to Jesus. Paul reminds Timothy that it is the inevitable lot of Christians (2 Timothy 3:12). The person who seeks to live a godly life will expose ungodliness, even though he may not necessarily have meant to (Ephesians 5:11). This may result in hostility.

For my own part I find the irrationality of hostility very painful and I am tempted to be ashamed of the gospel. Although Christians are commanded to be kind,

loving and gentle people (Galatians 5:22), and although
they are to do their evangelism with gentleness and
respect (1 Peter 3:16), often they will still be rejected for
no reason than the same one as their Lord (John 15:25).

Although he refers primarily to wayward believers,
Paul reminds us all, through his words to Timothy, that
we must not retaliate by being quarrelsome, nor yet with-
hold the gospel from those who seem to be hostile, as we
never know when God will grant them repentance (2
Timothy 2:24-26).

I do not think it is possible to engage in regular
evangelism whether directly such as speaking or indi-
rectly by living Christianly and expect to be popular.
Consequently popularity must not be elevated to a virtue
or a prerequisite for effective evangelism. So often
Christians have set out to make friends with people and
to cultivate good relationships, but for fear of losing
them, have failed to love their new friends sufficiently to
tell them the gospel. God has not treated *us* like that (Acts
17:30). I commend the making of good relationships. It is
essential for Christian behaviour, and so is evangelism.

There are strong reasons to be ashamed of the gospel.
Because of this I need to avail myself of the fellowship of
Christians who will encourage me not to give up in
evangelism. I need to know that Christian friends are
praying for me and therefore it is essential to have some
opportunity to tell them about those I am trying to lead
to Christ. It might be necessary, if your local church
doesn't provide this, for the Christian person to start
some small ad-hoc group for mutual encouragement and
support, and to warn of the danger of being ashamed
(Mark 8:38). I feel that it is unhelpful to encourage people
to engage in evangelism, to give them training in how to
do it, and not have them linked into some support/
nurture group.

Ashamed of the gospel?
I have always been intrigued by Paul's statement, "I am
not ashamed of the gospel" (Romans 1:16), and have
wondered why he felt it necessary to assure the Romans of

that fact. It seems such a strange statement to make! Would they have suspected that he *was* ashamed of the gospel? Probably not. However, because he is human, as we are, he *is* tempted to be ashamed and he knows the Romans are, so he gives them good reasons why he is not and why they shouldn't be either.

The gospel works

As I have already hinted, Paul tells us the reasons why he is not ashamed of the gospel and why he is eager to preach it at Rome (Romans 1:15).

Firstly, he reminds us that the gospel is the "power of God for salvation" (Romans 1:16). He is not ashamed of the Gospel because it works. It is the powerful way by which God brings people to salvation. Most people who become Christians do so through responding to the preaching of the gospel. That response may have taken place over a long period of time or in a moment. It may have been arrived at gradually through teaching in childhood, or by a swift conversion in adulthood, but whatever the process it was through the gospel.

Our own experience of the gospel should give us good heart to believe that others will become Christians through the same gospel. Although the unbeliever may think the gospel weak and foolish we have experienced its power. It is the way God brings men and women to faith (Romans 10:17). It may look feeble, but it is in fact powerful because it is about Jesus who has conquered death. God says it is the powerful way He uses to bring people to Himself. I am apt to forget that God is at work and that He works through the gospel. It is not my ability to persuade people in the end which changes them, but God.

The gospel is right

Secondly, Paul tells us the gospel shows us God's righteousness. Only in the gospel can be found the answer to the question "How can God act rightly and say I am acceptable to Him when I am sinful and unacceptable to Him?''. The answer lies in Jesus who died and rose again that I might be made acceptable 'in Him'. This is a great theme of the Epistle to the Romans. Such is the gospel that we do not need to pretend either about God's holiness, His righteousness, His fair dealing or about the extent of our sinfulness. Many try to resolve the problem apart from the gospel but only succeed in denying the truth. This is done by allowing God to tolerate our sinfulness, which would of course, reduce God to a person of complete carelessness about everything in His world. Conversely, it is done by reducing the seriousness of man's sin and thus minimising it completely. However, the gospel does neither. It shows God passionately concerned about our forgiveness and fellowship. It shows God loving us so much, He sends His Son to die so we could be forgiven (John 3:16; 1 John 2:1,2).

The gospel is powerful and right and there is no real reason to be ashamed of it. To be so, is diabolical and as such, needs to be resisted.

Some practical helps for evangelists.

1. Pray for boldness: (Acts 4:29; Ephesians 6:20). This is dealt with in more detail in chapter twelve, *Power for Evangelism.*

2. Seek fellowship support: Ask your Christian friends to pray for you (Colossians 4:2), and meet with them for prayer about the work you are involved in.

3. Work with others: It is a personal responsibility, but it often helps to work with someone else. You can give each other courage and support.

4. Know what to say: Skill in knowing what to say and how to say it, is a great help in overcoming fear. Part two of this book sets out some practical ways to evangelise and to train others to do the same.

Part 2

Knowing How

CHAPTER TEN

Person-to-Person Evangelism

Several years ago we in the Department of Evangelism for which I work considered making some television programmes. The cost of the proposal was so high that our budget for the whole year would have been used in the first month.

We sought the advice of a specialist in marketing, and were told: "No one who had the manpower which you have available would ever spend money on television advertising. They would use the money to train people to talk to other people about the product."

So we did—and so should your church, fellowship or Christian group. This chapter deals with the principles which govern this method of evangelism.

We are all called upon to be engaged in evangelism and most of us do this on the person-to-person basis. Some of the basic principles are outlined here. It is one of the most important aspects of evangelism. I often ask groups of Christians how they were led to Christ and more than half tell me they were converted through the ministry of a friend in the person-to-person situation.

Be prepared
We live in an age where spontaneity has been elevated to a prime virtue. Many think that if something happens that way it is more likely to be of the Holy Spirit than that which has been carefully planned. This is nonsense. Preparation for personal evangelism should be done in three areas.

1. Preparation of a godly life. This area is probably the most important of all. Observing the gospel being lived out in a godly life, will make people enquire as to why it is so!

If the gospel has not 'grabbed' me, then there is no reason why I should expect it will 'grab' others. However, if it is daily changing my life, it will give me great confidence to believe that the same gospel will change the lives of those to whom I tell it.

The whole purpose of life is to reflect God's character (Genesis 1:26; Romans 8:29). The reason why God called us back to Himself was so that we would be "holy and blameless in his sight" (Ephesians 1:4). The ministry of the Lord Jesus in raising us from the death of sin to new life was directed towards our doing "good works, which God prepared in advance for us to do" (Ephesians 2:10). We all need to pay special attention to this area of our lives. Reading and obeying the Bible, regular prayer, attendance at church with God's people are God-given ways to grow like Christ. This is expanded further in the section 'Training in Godliness'.

2. Prepare to know the gospel and explain it. No one who feels that he doesn't know what to say will ever try to speak about Jesus. In fact the gospel needs to be known so well that we don't need to think it out. Our thinking should be devoted to the person with whom we are speaking, listening carefully to him, and then knowing the best way to tell him the gospel. None of this can be done if all our thinking needs to be devoted to the content of the gospel. Some people have suggested to me that preparing like this may hinder the Holy Spirit from guiding us in that moment as to how we will answer.

I do not doubt at all that the Holy Spirit will guide us in such a situation—but we should not use that fact to allow us to become lazy and not learn what has been given to us by God, His gospel (Romans 1:1). Nor should we drive a wedge between the Bible—God's Word, and its author—God's Holy Spirit, as if they could somehow be opposed to each other. This gospel not only needs to be learned so that it can be recalled with ease, but also expressed with flexibility; in simple, relevant language;

and non-technical terms. In the next chapter there are two gospel outlines clearly set out and which I have used in personal evangelism. They may be helpful for you.

3. *Be prepared to answer questions.* Over a period of twelve years the Department of Evangelism in Sydney conducted hundreds of home dialogue meetings where non-Christians and Christians met for question and discussion. We kept a list of the questions which were asked in over 500 meetings, and those which were asked consistently were: "How do you know God exists?" "Are the New Testament documents reliable?" "Why does God allow suffering/wars, etc.?" "What about those who have never heard the gospel?" "Aren't all religions just different ways to get back to God?" "Do you have to go to church to be a Christian?" "Isn't faith psychological?" "Aren't all good people Christians?"

I was interested to see in Paul Little's *"How to Give Away your Faith"* (IVP, London) that these are substantially the same questions which he was asked most frequently on university campuses. His book has a brief but helpful chapter on some suggested answers to these questions.

Since personal evangelism is done with people, it stands to reason that we need to be where people are. We need to be in a sufficiently close relationship with them to be able to speak freely. Unfortunately a lot of Christians I know are so busy at church and with their Christian friends that they do not have any time left to meet people. Why do we organise so many church based clubs, sporting and otherwise, when we would make such good contacts as well as providing us with enjoyable activities if we joined non-church ones? When I went to 'Weight Watchers' I both gained and lost! I had a great time speaking to people personally about faith in Christ and I lost weight too—considerably!

Research done recently in the church growth movement has highlighted the fact that the average Christian has 'lost' most of his non-Christian friends within five years of becoming a Christian. There are some very good reasons why this takes place but often we exclude our old friends by our new 'exclusiveness'. Since we know this is so, we must take positive steps to deliberately find ways to reverse the trend. To take steps to join non-church organised groups will not only give us contact with new non-church members, but will also give us new insights into the way non-churchgoers think about life. Without first hand knowledge we tend to make assumptions, which are often wide of the mark. Such activities will take up a considerable amount of time and we may need to review our programme to allow the time for it. Often we have been so busy at church activities that we have allowed no time to be with *people*.

Start speaking

If we are to engage in personal evangelism we have to learn to be conversationalists. Very few people rush up to you and say "Good sir, what must I do to be saved?" However, if someone ever does, make sure you do not muck up that occasion! It happens that way so rarely!

Telling someone about Jesus is done in the context of a conversation which has already started and also in the context of a relationship which is friendly. We need to learn to initiate conversation.

Speaking to people in public varies from culture to culture. On a visit to the United Kingdom, I went for an early morning walk. It was a beautiful morning and as I walked along a man came jogging towards me. "Good morning," I said. He stopped in his tracks—stared at me, obviously trying to remember where we had met, (we hadn't). "Beautiful morning isn't it?" I tried again. He now seemed so embarrassed that I just moved on. I didn't know if it was personal or cultural, so I thought I would try again. To the next jogger I said, "Great morning isn't it?"

"Sure is" came the reply in the broadest American drawl! So I still don't know the answer, but suspect it was cultural.

The Christian way to approach somebody is to do it in a way we would like them to approach us. How do we know if people want us to speak to them? We need to experiment and see. When a man sits next to me in the

train I close my paper, smile at him and say, "Good day".
He usually indicates, in an unmistakable way, if he
wishes the conversation to proceed or stop. If he answers
in a mono-syllabic grunt, opens his paper and begins to
read, that seems clear guidance to me. I open mine again
and read. If he starts speaking, I take it he wants to, so I
listen and make contributions. I know it is in the context
of speaking that I might be able to say something
Christian with a view to getting around to the gospel.
Such a conversation needs to be backed up with prayer, so
I start praying. If we get around to Christian matters—
well and good. If we don't, I do not worry because I know
that the sovereign God is able to keep the conversation
alive until I have said all God wants me to say on that
occasion.

I remember the day that I picked up two hitchhikers.
One in the morning and one later in the day. I got into
friendly and enjoyable conversation with both and I was
able to share the gospel with one. With the other it didn't
seem appropriate to do so within any of the things we
discussed. I was *willing* to share the gospel with both. I
had *prayed* for both men as they got in and during the
conversation. With one it seemed the most natural thing
to do. With the other, every time I vaguely moved towards
saying something Christian the conversation took a
different turn Can I trust the sovereign God in both
situations? I can, and in both cases I did. Rejoicing that
both opportunities had come my way, I committed both
situations to God in prayer. I sought to be obedient to
God on both occasions and I had treated both men like
persons and not like things.

The weather or the gospel?

However, we still need to give serious thought to how to
get around to Christian truths. It is possible to talk about
the weather and the football indefinitely but never get
around to any matters of substance, and if we are ever
going to do so again we will have to take the initiative.
Sometimes with friends we know well we may have to say
quite directly "We have never really spoken about

Christian matters, I wonder if I could tell you about Jesus sometime?" or "How far do you think you have got in your pilgrimage to God?" I think that such a direct approach can be used where we are known and trusted, and where we have taken the time to build a relationship.

Related to this direct approach is what I call 'God talk'. When someone says "I saw your bishop on T.V. last night". I never say, "What was he like?" which I've found often leads nowhere, but something like "Did he say anything about Jesus?" If on the other hand I had seen the programme, I would say "I thought the point he made about...was very impressive" and I would head straight for the gospel.

When the man next to you at work tells you that his wife has cancer, you may well say something like "You must be terribly worried. My wife goes to a prayer group on Tuesdays. Would you mind if they prayed for you both?"

When asked "What sort of a weekend did you have?", instead of saying "Oh, it was good", try "We heard a terrific sermon on Sunday night", and see where it leads.

Personal evangelism is not like preaching a sermon one-to-one. It is much more like 'verbal scrabble'! I say something, he answers, I respond to his answer, etc. I know what I want to say ultimately—the gospel. Whether I am able to do so is largely governed by what he says to me and whether the gospel is appropriate in the conversation we are having. Because of this I need to develop more and more a Christian world view so that when we are speaking about life in general I have something Christian to say.

To do this I 'trained' for a year with a friend. We decided to read the editorial in a daily newspaper and to ask this question: "If someone begins speaking about this subject what can I say which is Christian and relevant?" We 'phoned each other every day and compared our thoughts. Sometimes one, or both would come up with something useful. At other times we were unable to say anything at all. The value of the exercise lay in the constant thinking in Christian categories of the world around us. Try the exercise yourself. What do your friends at work talk about? Can you say anything distinctively Christian on that subject. If you can, then when the conversation comes up again, as others make *their* contribution, make *yours* and see where it leads. Don't make a big thing out of it—just make it. You may find you will be asked to give a reason. This in turn may lead to the gospel. Don't lose any sleep if it doesn't. Try again on some other topic or on that one again some other time. Keep practising—the first fifty years are the hardest! Remember you do not have to say everything at once. You will get other opportunities and you are not the only Christian they will meet.

Some examples

The following incidents happened to me. They illustrate what I am saying. Since you are not me nor I you, you may well have answered differently. The way we proceed in conversation is almost as individualistic as a tooth-brush. Some of you will say, "Is that the best he can do?" Others will say, "I couldn't do that!" Those of you who are like I am may find them useful, but don't copy me, teach yourself to think Christianly about life.

The first conversation took place one night when I was putting out my dustbin. A neighbour pointed out that vandals had chopped down several shrubs in the park opposite. He was very angry about it. I admit I was none too pleased myself.

"What a hopeless action that is," he said.

"We had better get used to it," I said. "I suspect it will get worse, not better."

"That's a fairly pessimistic view," he answered.

"It's inevitable I think."

"It's crazy behaviour."

"When you say 'goodbye' to God," I said; "it is difficult to teach people not to give full expression to anything they want to do. '

"I don't believe in God and I don't chop down trees," he said.

"Why shouldn't the person who did it do it if he feels like it?"

"Because the rest of us cannot enjoy them."

"But why should he worry about us," I pressed.

"Because that is how we ought to live."

"Who says so?" I answered. "I agree with you, but I do so because God says so. But if it is just a matter of your opinion plus my opinion versus the vandal's opinion, I cannot see why ours is right and his is wrong. Only God is able to make statements about what is ultimately right and wrong."

From here the conversation moved into the general area of the existence of God and to the person of the Lord Jesus. Much more profitable than the park and the vandals!

The second incident took place during a time of political upheaval in Australia. Everyone was talking about it. I was driving home from the country and gave a lift to a university undergraduate who was also a scientist. He was returning from holidays. Naturally we spoke about the government and the elections. "It is very difficult in the western world, at present, to be a leader," I said.

"Do you think it is more difficult now than before?" he asked.

"Much! In the past we believed in absolutes and so we agreed on what was right and wrong. Now a leader makes a statement on one issue and people flock to him. He makes another statement and they all rush away to another leader. We have lost our 'body of truth' and do not seem to know how to arrive at truth."

"I don't believe that sort of truth exists. I don't think there are any absolutes," he said.

"Surely that statement is an absolute," I responded.

"Well, I believe *that* is the only absolute," he replied.

"Where did you get it from?" I asked.

"It's what I live by."

"Surely it is God's role to make up the absolutes."

We had a long and fruitful conversation about the existence of God and the Lord Jesus.

A careful answer
Paul gives this advice to the Colossians. "Be wise in the way you act toward outsiders; make the most of every opportunity. Let your conversation be always full of grace, seasoned with salt, so that you may know how to answer everyone" (Colossians 4:5,6). Our conversations are to be loving, penetrating and appropriate. No wonder he asked them to pray for him, their leader. Let me urge you to pray for your teacher so in time *you* will be able to answer in such a way.

Often in the life situation we find ourselves only able to make a brief comment. We don't have much time to think. Perhaps a work colleague looks worried—"What's the matter, Tom?" "We learned yesterday that our boy Jack is on heroin. I'm terribly worried." What will I say? "I generally ask God to help me to act wisely with my kids. Would you like me to pray for you?" We all need more skill in 'knowing how to answer everyone'. We need to pray and to keep thinking about the world around us as God does. Which is another way of saying 'keep thinking about the world like the Bible does'.

Like an oyster
I remember the most popular address given at a Speech Day at our school was delivered by a local politician. He was last on a very long list of speakers. "I have always thought the oyster had a great deal going for it," he began. "It always knows when to shut up." With that he sat down!!! The applause was sustained and deafening.

If the hardest part in personal evangelism is getting around to saying something Christian, the next most difficult aspect is to know when to stop. In my own case I am so relieved and excited to be able to share Jesus that I tend to go on and on. What guidelines are there to follow?

Once again I think it is worth stating that we are in conversation which is dialogue not monologue. At all times during the conversation we should be seeking to be sensitive to the signs which show when the other person no longer wishes to continue the discussion. Sometimes this can be noticed by a look or by an answer. I may not be sure and may need to say something like "We might be able to speak about this some other time". This sensitivity comes from God and His Holy Spirit as we carefully observe the person with whom we are speaking. To that end we need to remind ourselves to act "full of grace" (Colossians 4:5,6) and we need to be much in prayer as we proceed. Remember God is well able to keep the conversation going for as long as we have everything to say which He wants us to say on that occasion. Sometimes we may be the first link in a chain of events which will lead that person to Christ. Sometimes we will be a middle link and sometimes we will be the last link and will find ourselves saying "Is there any real reason why you should not turn to Christ now". Don't prejudge the situations. We do not know all the circumstances, but God does. That truth is so encouraging.

Something to read

I usually carry in my wallet a small tract which I can give away when it seems appropriate after a conversation. Sometimes a book on a particular subject might be more appropriate. I tend to lend a book rather than give it, then I can pursue the conversation when it is returned. Read the book yourself before you give it to someone so that you are able to talk about it. I often underline key parts in it so that when the book is returned I can say "This quote on page twenty-seven is impressive, isn't it?" rather than "What did you think about it?" (which I have always found leads nowhere).

Start now

The hardest part in all evangelism is starting. We will do almost anything except begin. We do another training course, read another book. We form yet another committee and even go to prayer meetings about it. But if you have not started—IT IS TIME. The best way to learn is to do it. None of us is much good at the beginning.

CHAPTER ELEVEN

Training Yourself and Others

This chapter is longer than the others, and it is presented in seven sections, each dealing with some aspect of training either yourself or others to be effective in evangelism.

One of the keys to continuous evangelism is effective training.

In an earlier chapter we concluded that it is the responsibility of the minister to see that training is made available to the members of the congregation. He may do it himself or use others.

You may find yourself in a situation where good training is available to you, but if this is not the case you should set to and train yourself. Someone must have done that at the beginning! On the other hand, you may find yourself in the position where you are called upon to train others.

The training course
Whether you are training yourself or others, the programme should cover the following major areas.

I A MODEL TO FOLLOW—GENERAL PRINCIPLES

II GROWTH IN CHRISTIAN LIVING

III INSTRUCTION IN AN EASILY MEMORISED GOSPEL OUTLINE

IV HOW TO ANSWER QUESTIONS RELATED TO THE GOSPEL OR LIFE

V   SELECTION OF SUITABLE METHODS
VI FINDING SPECIAL METHODS FOR INDIVID-
    UALS
VII INSTRUCTION ON NURTURE GROUPS

I   A MODEL TO FOLLOW

General Principles to adopt

Let us suppose we are setting up some training course for a group of people. Some of the areas of training listed, e.g. the gospel outline, answering questions and follow-up nurture can be done individually or in groups. Finding a suitable method to use needs to be done on an individual basis.

(a) Demonstration versus instruction. Suppose we are running a course on door-to-door visiting and have given some basic teaching on the gospel and on the questions people are likely to ask. We have been stressing all the time, the need for holiness of life. We now come to some basic instruction about actually making the calls. We need to answer questions like, "What will I say when the door opens?" "How will I introduce myself?" "How will I tell them why I'm there and what I'd like to do?" This can be followed by role-plays with people taking various parts. The question then arises, when is the 'trained' person ready to begin?

The *Evangelism Explosion*, D.J. Kennedy's training system, and the *Navigators* have shown that the best training is on-the-spot practical demonstration. The trainer actually takes the trainee with him and does the door-to-door visit. He is seen in action applying the principles about which he has been speaking. After the visit they are able to analyse what was done and why. This should be repeated until the trainee has enough confidence to speak as they continue visiting together. The trainer is able to see whether the trainee has really understood the principles and can put them into action. It also allows him to make suggestions about varying the method. The ultimate aim is that the trainee will become a trainer of others and he will do that in the way he himself was trained.

(b) Versatility in method. People are different and vary greatly in their abilities, therefore methods need to be matched with the different people who can use them. However, I am convinced that even within any one method, variations will need to be made for individual differences. The temptation to bypass this training is very strong because it is so time consuming. Most of us want quicker returns for our training times. However, the lasting results when such training time is spent carefully, are very impressive, especially if every trainee ultimately becomes a trainer.

Unfortunately many of us have experienced those training schemes where we were only told *what* to do. We practised in the role-play situation and were sent out to do the job. The difference between the real life situation and the role-play was even greater than we had imagined or were led to believe. Some people survived and continued. Those who were badly hurt felt guilty and withdrew from the team. That was bad enough but generally they came to the conclusion that they could not evangelise anyone, so didn't try again with that method or any other method either. What is even worse, some were not able to find relief for their guilt and were robbed of the joy of actually engaging in evangelism. In a door-to-door visitation programme some may be able to talk quite easily about the gospel—others invite people to a meeting—others give away some printed material. The level will be determined as the individual makes calls initially with his trainer. All who have consistently engaged in any method know how they have modified the techniques which they were taught so that the training method could be used easily.

It will happen in a training programme that some people may need to be encouraged *NOT* to proceed with a given technique because they cannot really use it. In such a case the trainer will need to find some other method so that the person can fulfil his obligation to engage in evangelism.

(c) Pastoral responsibility. Whoever trains people to use any evangelistic technique must take pastoral responsibility for that person not only during the initial

stages, but in the ongoing programme. Those who engage in any ongoing programmes of evangelism know that some visits are good, others not so good and others are most generously described as disappointing. The experienced worker knows of this wide variety and so does not give up after a disappointing venture. The trainee has no such background of experience so he will need to be encouraged by his trainer as together they find the best way to use the method chosen. Our ultimate aim for all people we train is that evangelism will become a way of life which they will continue all their lives.

If this is to happen we will need to set up some 'nurture' group where the joy in the work can be shared, disappointments prayed about, 'wounds licked' and perseverance encouraged. Most Christians cannot sustain their zeal indefinitely without the help of others, nor should we expect them to do so.

Although I have stated that evangelism is a personal responsibility that does not mean that we must always do it by ourselves. There is a very real value in doing evangelism in pairs or small groups. Not only do we get encouragement but we actually do more. A friend told me how he was involved in a group project where it was decided to approach new students enrolling at a university to invite them to lunch and to talk to them about Jesus. My friend had arranged to do this with a friend but when he arrived at the enrolment office, his friend hadn't turned up. Although there were plenty of students enrolling, he 'chickened out' and did nothing. The moment the friend arrived he said, "Great to see you, let's get started" and they immediately issued an invitation—which was accepted. Alone it was too difficult. With another he actually took the initiative, began, and encouraged his friend to do the same.

(d) *Realistic expectations*. If the trainer doesn't do the work himself as well as teach it, he will forget as time goes by how difficult it is and unconsciously he may raise false expectations in those who are being trained. He may not mean to do this, but it will occur.

In an endeavour to recruit more people to enrol in training courses the 'success' stories are often told but the others are neglected. It is a good idea to keep some records so that the true picture can be told.

I discussed this with a person who was doing evangelism through a home Bible study course.

People were recruited by a visitation programme and they were invited to join the group for a six week period. Five non-church attenders out of every two hundred homes visited joined the group. Knowing a fact like that can help us not to be too disappointed when we don't enrol ten from the first ten visits.

For several years we ran home meetings which we called 'Dialogue Evangelism' meetings. A host couple asked their non-church attending friends to come to an evening to discuss Christianity. Consistently we found that only three-quarters of those who said they would come, in fact came. We also found we had an average taken over five hundred meetings, of seven non-church attenders each night. That kind of information will help the host and hostess to have realistic expectations. I do not wish to limit the power of the Holy Spirit, nor do I want people to be of 'little faith'. However, the person who trains others needs to consider whether he has built into the training programme proper helps which will enable his trainee to continue indefinitely in the work of evangelism.

Refresher courses

Exactly the way in which we tend to refine and alter a technique to suit ourselves, it is possible to slip into unhelpful ways, which if practised become permanent without our noticing it. Consequently refresher courses should be available.

In 1976 I was visiting England and I trained a group of leaders in Dialogue Evangelism. I returned in 1980 and was leading a series of Dialogue Meetings. One of the men who had trained in 1976 and had used the method extensively over the four year period, pointed out to me that I had made some substantial variations to the method. Frankly I was unaware that I had, but when he pointed them out I was able to recognise them. Some were valuable changes, others were not and needed to be modified. It needed someone more objective than I was to recognise them.

This probably applies to us all, and to our methods of teaching. Take a long hard *objective* look at the method you are using. Does it need a few changes?

II   TRAINING IN CHRISTIAN GROWTH

Whether you are training yourself or training others, the training programme must begin with godly living. Evangelism is never a matter of simply learning the right techniques. Because it is part of the Christian life it should flow from the life which is given over to God and in service to Him.

It is not without significance that, although the disciples were called and commissioned with the words "Come, follow me and I will make you fishers of men" (Matthew 4:19), it was really quite a time before they were sent out on their mission (Matthew 10:5-10). There is no doubt that the nature of their call was to follow Jesus and in doing so to become "fishers of men"! Their response was immediate and total (Matthew 4:20,21), and it was followed by the Sermon on the Mount (Matthew chapters 5 to 7) where they were given careful instructions in what it means to live as a member of the Kingdom of heaven, which is another way of saying they were given instruction in godly living.

Why is it so important to stress this matter?

First, it is the whole purpose of our being called back to God. Paul tells us that "those God foreknew he also predestined to be conformed to the likeness of his Son" (Romans 8:29). To grow like Christ is to be truly human. It is fundamentally what life is all about. It will be hard to persuade someone that this is so if it is obviously not the aim of your life, or the way you are living.

Second, if godliness is not the aim of your life, you will engage in evangelistic methods which do not reflect the character of God. The method will not be like the message. We have all been subjected to people who have embarrassed every one, including us, at college or at work by their constant 'sermons', their complete insensitivity to others, accompanied by neglect of their work, their friends and their family. When they have finished speaking the rest of us are left to pick up the pieces and try to repair the broken relationships.

From time to time a man walked up and down outside a church in our city bellowing out the gospel to everyone who passed by and others who were sitting in a square nearby, (although I noticed the numbers diminished on the days he performed).

He always sounded aggressive and most times he could not be understood as he was forced to bellow so loudly above the traffic noise! Several times he invited me to join him, but I declined and suggested that a more effective way to evangelise would be to start up friendly conversations with people in the square, asking them if he might share the gospel with them. He was not impressed by my alternative. He said it would be less effective because he would 'reach' so few by that method. My own view is that the suggestion was far too difficult for him to contemplate.

The gospel he was expounding may have been 'reaching' a lot of people, but it is doubtful whether many of them were 'receiving' it.

When I see (and hear!) that type of person in action, I cringe inwardly because the *method* is so unlike the *message*.

When the method and the message are at strong variance, not only does the behaviour of the person make it difficult for people to hear the message, but other Christians are embarrassed and are also discouraged from speaking about their own Christian faith. They tend to swing to the opposite extreme and make up their minds not to speak at all in case they appear to others to be 'rat-bags'. Part of the solution is to live a godly life of love, gentleness and sensitivity. In such a context speaking as opportunities arise will seem quite natural. This blend of method and message makes a powerful combination.

A powerful combination
One evening after an evangelistic service, I counselled a husband and wife who had been converted that morning. Here is the story the wife told me. "I was in hospital having just given birth to twins. I had two other children under school age and was worried about how I would cope when I got home. A stranger arrived one day and said, 'I'm Mary...and I come from St Phillip's Church. We heard about you through a friend and the ladies at our church would like to help when you come home. We could work out a roster so that each morning through the week one of us will come straight after breakfast and leave after lunch, if that's all right with you'. They came and washed, cleaned, ironed and prepared an evening meal before they left in mid-afternoon. They did it for twelve months! We were very glad of their help. Both my husband and I thought it wouldn't last but after three months my husband said 'We ought to go to church to see what makes them like that'. So we went and have realised now that it is really Jesus who makes them like they are, and today we decided to become His followers also".

It was a very moving story, as was the behaviour of the St Phillip's ladies. Real love is very hard to disguise. It was the *living* which brought them to the *preaching* and the *preaching* which brought them to Christ.

Many of you may know those very powerful words of Gertrude Behanna on her record "God is Not Dead" (Word Records). She tells how she had been invited to dinner to meet some Christian friends of the host. She says she was so frightened by the prospect that she drank herself into semi-oblivion and behaved quite stupidly with them. They behaved with love and charm. After a day or so she received a letter in which they said that they had been glad to meet her—they were sending a booklet under separate cover—they thought she might like to read it—if she had time. She says, "It was my first introduction to the courtesy of Christ". She had time—she read it and was converted. It is a very moving record. Their kindness and thoughtfulness *pointed* to the book. The book *pointed* to Christ and faith came through hearing about Him (Romans 10:17).

During the last ten years I have spoken at hundreds of small meetings in homes. There is no doubt in my mind that some of the hardest people to reach with the gospel are those who have been hurt by Christians (or church members). One man told how he'd been swindled in a business deal by a church warden. "Do you want me to become like him?" he asked. "I want both you and him to become like Jesus" was the only reply I could think of. But I grieved over that situation.

A good model

Saint Paul is a good model to follow. He tells the Corinthians "we have renounced secret and shameful ways: We do not use deception, nor do we distort the word of God. On the contrary, by setting forth the truth plainly we commend ourselves to every man's conscience in the sight of God...For we do not preach ourselves, but Jesus Christ as Lord, and ourselves as your servants for Jesus' sake" (2 Corinthians 4:2,4). He is against any behaviour which is inconsistent with the message. He knows that people cannot be 'conned' into the kingdom so he tells them the truth about Jesus and he does it as their servant.

We may be tempted to say "I'll have to wait until my life becomes more Christ-like before I say anything!" Two things need to be said. First, God is able to overrule our mistakes (see Philippians 1:15-18) and second, speaking openly is part of growing like Christ. We cannot become more Christ-like by waiting. We need to take action. Peter tells us to reverence Christ in our hearts as Lord and to be ready at all times to make a defence for being a Christian, doing so with "gentleness and respect, keeping a clear conscience" (1 Peter 3:16).

The message and the life are not to contradict each other.

What leads to godliness?

It is the work of the Holy Spirit to transform us into the likeness of Christ (2 Corinthians 3:18). God has promised that He will complete this work (Romans 8:28-30) and the knowledge of this should fill us with wonder and cause us to be willing to co-operate with Him in this work. There are several ways which God has provided for us to grow in the Christian life. The study of the Bible, praying, fellowshipping with other Christians and evangelism are all means which God has provided for us. Whether we are training ourselves or others, we need to check on these areas of growth in our own lives as well as encouraging others to do so in theirs.

(a) *The study of the Bible*. God has given us His Word the Bible, so that we might know what He is like and how we should live in fellowship with Him. It is a book which points us to the Lord Jesus. On one occasion Jesus said to the Pharisees "You diligently study the scriptures because you think that by them you possess eternal life. These are the scriptures that testify about me" (John 5:39). As we read the Bible we learn about God and what pleases Him so that we are able to cultivate an ongoing relationship with Him by doing the things which please Him. This is the way all relationships work.

If I don't know you I don't know how to please you. Suppose you and I are at supper in the church hall and I see you without anything to drink. I bring you a cup of tea. "Thank you," you say. "I normally drink coffee but I can drink tea. However, I generally have my tea without milk but never mind, I can drink it with milk."

"I've put sugar in it," I say.

"That's finished it! I cannot drink tea with sugar."

Although I aimed to please you, I did not know how to please you because I did not really know you, or what you liked.

The Bible should be studied obediently. Jesus said, "If you love me, you will do what I command" (John 14:15). To do what is pleasing to God is to demonstrate our love for Him. So the study of the Bible is not an end in itself, it is the means whereby we get to know God and to show our love by obeying Him.

The Bible should be studied regularly. The Psalmist says that the happy man is the man whose "...delight is in the law of the Lord, and on his law he meditates day and night" (Psalm 1:2). He is only able to do this because he knows the Scriptures. They require regular study. The person who reads the Bible every day is likely to read more than the one who reads it spasmodically. The habit of setting aside a time each day when we can be alone with God in Bible study and prayer is to be commended. An alarm clock is a helpful investment in this matter! The best time is when we are not too tired to take in what we are reading. The choice of time should reflect the importance we place on growing in Christ-likeness.

The Bible should be studied systematically. Not only should we read the Bible regularly, but we should aim to read it systematically. Try to read through the Bible at least once each year. If we were to read four chapters a day we could read the Old Testament once and the New Testament twice each year. Why not make up a daily reading programme for yourself? Alternatively, the Bible Society has a plan available to read through the Bible annually, and the Scripture Union has excellent Bible reading plans and helpful notes.

The Bible should be studied with others. As well as reading the Bible privately, we have all been helped by reading it with other people. They are able to share their insights with us, and together we can encourage each other to obey God's Word.

The Bible should be studied humbly and prayerfully. The Bible is not a book which requires us to be clever in order to understand it. The Holy Spirit is the author of the Bible (2 Peter 1:21; 2 Timothy 3:16; John 14:26) and He is our teacher. Consequently we need to come humbly to the Bible praying that He will teach us how to understand it so that we may obey it. Ultimately it is the obedient person who will understand the Bible rather than the clever one who does not obey (John 7:17).

If you are training yourself, it would be a good idea to review your Bible reading habits and if there is need to start again, then do so.

If you are training others they will find it helpful if you share with them your own Bible reading habits and have them share with each other. This whole area is of vital importance and should not be either underestimated or taken for granted.

Linked with the study of the Bible is prayer.

(b) Prayer. We study the Bible so that we can get to know God more and enjoy fellowship with Him. Prayer is the God given way for us to speak with Him and cultivate close fellowship with Him.

Most Christians have found it helpful to set aside a special time in the day for prayer so that it is not neglected, but prayer need not be restricted to this. During a day most of us engage in routine activity which requires very little thinking, such as washing up or walking to the bus stop. These can be useful times to pray. Sometimes prayer is spontaneous as in moments of great joy or sorrow, when a sudden crisis arises, or when an important decision is to be made quickly. Such is the wonder of the death of Jesus on our behalf that we can come confidently into God's presence with our requests (Hebrews 10:19,22), and we are encouraged to do so (1 Thessalonians 5:17; Ephesians 6:18-20; James 4:16-18). It would be helpful if your group studied these passages as well as some of the great prayers which we have in the Bible (Ephesians 3:14-21; Matthew 9:35-38; Luke 11:1-10; Daniel 9:4-19; Psalm 51; 1 Kings 18:36,37).

Our prayer times should include thanksgiving (Philippians 4:6); confession (1 John 1:7); intercession for others as well as ourselves (1 Timothy 2:1,2); and special prayer for the spread of the gospel (Colossians 4:2). Many Christians have found it helpful to keep a prayer diary so that certain people and events are prayed for on certain days. The advantage is that they are not forgotten over the passage of time.

Because both Bible study and prayer are so helpful in our Christian growth, we can be certain that Satan will do everything he can to deflect us from doing them regularly. He is to be resisted in this regard. When he is resisted, we have the promise that God will draw near to us as we do to Him (James 4:7,8). When training others we need to warn them not to be surprised when they find they are tempted to neglect prayer and Bible study, and we must encourage them to persist with both.

In calling us to grow like Jesus, God has not only provided us with the Bible and prayer, but also given us Christian brothers and sisters to help us.

(c) Fellowshipping with the church. The Christians, to whom the Epistle to the Hebrews was written, were beginning to forget how important the fellowship of God's people was and they were neglecting church. The writer needed to exhort them, "And let us consider" he said, "how we may spur one another on towards love and good deeds. Let us not give up meeting together, as some are in the habit of doing, but let us encourage one another" (Hebrews 10:24,25).

God never envisaged that we will grow Christ-like without helping others and being helped by them. God has designed the Church as a meeting where we can be taught the Bible and minister our gifts to others and be ministered to by them. The Bible knows nothing of isolated Christians who refuse to fellowship with others (Ephesians 4:1-13).

We all need to be encouraged not to neglect each other and this should not be overlooked in the training course. We should be encouraged to look for ways to minister to each other as well as being ministered to. This can be done informally as well as formally.

(d) Telling others. Finally, one of the God-given ways to Christian growth is that of evangelism. The sharing of the gospel itself is a Christ-like activity. He is the One who came to seek and to save the lost (Luke 19:10). Paul tells us that he lived the way he did so that he was able to take the gospel to the maximum number of people, and in so doing share in the benefits of the gospel (1 Corinthians 9:19-23).

It should be pointed out in a training programme that godliness is an essential for evangelism and evangelism is essential for godliness.

Christ-likeness of character is the reason why God called us back to Himself. It is what life really is all about. Christ-likeness is also essential if we are to engage in evangelism, and not display behaviour which is at variance with the message. Finally it is imperative that the person who leads others to Christ can teach how to grow in Christ-likeness and become a mature Christian. He cannot teach this if he has not learned it himself.

Paul's words to Timothy are a timely reminder to us all.

"Have nothing to do with godless myths and old wives' tales; rather train yourself to be godly. For physical training is of some value, but godliness has value for all things, holding promise for both the present life and the life to come" (1 Timothy 4:7,8).

III   A GOSPEL OUTLINE

Although most Christians know about the gospel and have heard many evangelistic sermons, it is still necessary to teach them a clear and simple gospel outline which can be learned and reproduced with ease and skill. Such an outline should:
(a) be able to be remembered easily
(b) be expressed in non-technical terms
(c) contain sufficient information to achieve a response
(d) be uncomplicated

In this section I have detailed and expanded two outlines which I have both used and taught to others. The first outline is one which I constructed myself, and the second is the expansion of a booklet, *2 Ways to Live*. Both are good statements of the gospel and both comply with the criteria listed above.

Outline number one
1. This is God's world. He made it and is in charge of it. God has declared His Son, Jesus to be Ruler over His world and we know this because Jesus rose again from the dead. Jesus has the right to run our lives.
2. Everyone is rebellious to the fact that Jesus should run their lives. They may express this in open hostility, or by passive indifference. In either case, the rebellion is real.

3. God calls on us to stop rebelling and to turn back and submit to Jesus as our rightful Ruler.

4. If a person does stop rebelling and turns back to submit to Jesus as his Ruler, he is treated as if he had never rebelled. He is forgiven because of the death of Jesus on his behalf.

5. If a person will not submit to Jesus, but continues to rebel, in the end he will be overthrown because Jesus really is Ruler in God's world, and the rightful Ruler in each person's life.

Non-technical terms

In this outline, technical terms such as sovereignty, sin, guilt, repentance, justification, propitiation, hell, etc., have been avoided.

One problem is that even when these words are in common usage, they rarely convey to people the meaning that they have in the Bible. For example, the word *sin* conveys to most people the idea of something gross such as murder. To call someone a *sinner* will almost always be interpreted as a character judgment in almost any part of the western world.

In this gospel outline, various phrases have been substituted for the technical terms listed, and the word *sin* has been substituted by the phrase *to rebel against the right of Jesus to rule over you.*

Guilt. Most people think of guilt as 'feeling guilty', so if they don't feel guilty they assume they are not. Guilt has been replaced by the phrase *all people have rebelled.*

Repentance is not just 'feeling sorry'. The alternative phrase used is, *God calls on us to stop rebelling and to submit to Jesus.*

Justify conveys to most people the idea of 'finding an excuse for your actions'. The phrase *he is treated as if he had never rebelled* is used instead of the word 'justify'.

Hell. Very few people seem to believe in hell and the word is not taken seriously today. To use the term recalls odd notions gathered from cartoons and is associated in most people's minds with jokes. The phrase *in the end he will be overthrown* has been substituted.

How to learn the outline

Remembering the outline will be easy if five headings are memorised:

1. God
2. Man
3. God
4. What if he does?
5. What if he won't?

Now, here is the suggested method and the steps involved in training yourself or others:

Step One. Explain the outline to the group, detailing the substituted words/phrases.

Step Two. Have the group write down in full, the gospel outline.

Step Three. Teach the five headings, and from these explain and teach the contents summarised below:

1. God	This is God's world, He made it.
	God has made Jesus ruler of his world, through His rising from the dead.
	Jesus has the right to control and run our lives.
2. Man	Everyone has rebelled against Jesus' right to run his/her life. Some in open hostility, others in passive apathy—it is real just the same.
3. God	Calls on us all to stop rebelling and to submit to Jesus.
4. What if he does?	If a person stops rebelling and submits to Jesus he is treated as if he had never rebelled.
5. What if he won't?	If a person won't submit to Jesus, in the end that person will be overthrown. Jesus really is in charge of God's world.

Step Four. Set up role-plays where this outline can be practised aloud until all can say it easily and naturally. This can be done in pairs or small groups.

Step Five. Have the members of the group find a Bible verse which is appropriate for each heading in the outline. These verses should be learned so that they can be introduced when and if they are needed. It is important that the verses be from the version of the Bible which the trainee will use in his evangelism. Confusion could result otherwise.

A sample set of verses could be:

1. God	Genesis 1:1; Philippians 2:9,11
2. Man	Romans 3:12; 1 John 3:4
3. God	Acts 17:30
4. What if he does?	John 3:16
5. What if he won't?	2 Thessalonians 1:8,9

Step Six. Encourage the members of the group to have available practical illustrations for at least two of the five headings in the outline.

Examples of illustrations

An illustration for the second heading. All people have rebelled against the right of Jesus to run their lives. Some people express it in open opposition, and others in passive indifference, but either way it is an expression of a rebellion which is real.

Suppose two of us were in an army unit and we both received an order from a superior. One is openly critical of the order and disobeys it. The other just ignores it. Neither of us obeys, but we demonstrate our rebellion to authority in different ways. Rebellion to Jesus' right to rule over us is similar; some are active in opposition, others just ignore Him.

An illustration for the fourth heading. What if a person does stop rebelling? What treatment would he receive if he decided to turn back and submit to Jesus?

I remember a boy telling me how when he was quite

young he and his brother ran away from home. They sat in a cave in the small valley behind their house until it was dark, then deciding that they had taught their father his lesson, they went back home. When their father saw them he rushed out and hugged them saying, "Hullo, you two. I thought you'd gone. Have you eaten?"

I was telling this story to a group when a young man said, "They were lucky. When I came home, my father half killed me!"

The question "What will God do?" is a good one. What will happen? Well, like those two runaway boys, I am treated *as if I'd never rebelled. I am forgiven* because Jesus has died for me.

The training session. How long, how often?

Sufficient time needs to be allowed for the memory work to be done, and for people to practise sufficiently to become completely familiar and conversant with the outline. Sessions of an hour a week for a six-week period will allow time between sessions for memorising and practising.

If you are training yourself to use this outline, you will need to work through the steps and the headings at your own pace. It is important to practise the outline aloud so that you can 'hear' how it sounds. It would be helpful to do this with a friend.

Outline number two

2 Ways to Live is an outline developed by the staff at St. Matthias' Anglican Church, Centennial Park, Sydney. It is available as a booklet from the Anglican Information Office, Sydney by whose permission it is reproduced here.

By using a set of six simple drawings, the person using the outline can remember the sequence and the content as it is presented to the hearer.

1.	2.	3.
4.	5.	6.

Preparation

Rule up a page as above, explaining as you do so that you will illustrate your points as you go.

Steps One to Six

The drawings are completed progressively in the numbered squares as each step is explained as follows:

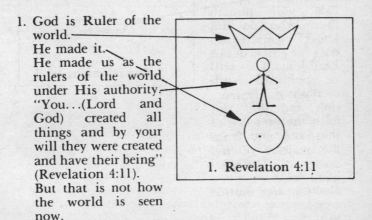

1. God is Ruler of the world.
He made it.
He made us as the rulers of the world under His authority.
"You...(Lord and God) created all things and by your will they were created and have their being" (Revelation 4:11).
But that is not how the world is seen now.

1. Revelation 4:11

2. We all reject God's authority over us. We want to run things by ourselves without God. But we can't control ourselves or society or the world. "...all have turned away, they have together become worthless" (Romans 3:12). What do you think God will do about such rebellion?

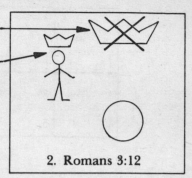

2. Romans 3:12

3. God will not allow men to continue to rebel against Him. God's punishment for rebellion is eternal death. "He will punish those who do not know God and do not obey the gospel of our Lord Jesus. They will be punished with everlasting destruction and shut out from the presence of the Lord and from the majesty of his power (2 Thessalonians 1:8,9). God's justice sounds very hard! But...

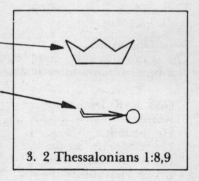

3. 2 Thessalonians 1:8,9

4. Because of His love, God sent His Son into our world, the man Jesus Christ. Jesus always lived under God's rule. But Jesus came to take our punishment for us by dying in our place. "He committed no sin..." (1 Peter 2:22). "He himself bore our sins in his body on the tree..." (1 Peter 2:24). But that is not all...

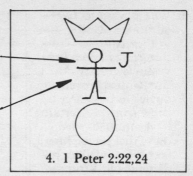

4. 1 Peter 2:22,24

5. God raised Jesus to life again which shows that Jesus
—conquered death
—is the Ruler of the universe
—is the giver of new life.
"In his great mercy he has given us new birth into a living hope through the resurrection of Jesus Christ from the dead" (1 Peter 1:3).
Where does this leave us?

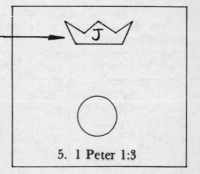

5. 1 Peter 1:3

6. The 2 ways to live—
   A. *Reject God's authority.
      *Run our own lives our own way.
      *Be disapproved by God.
      *Facing certain death.
   B. *Trust Jesus Christ.
      *Acknowledge Jesus as our King.
      *Forgiven by God.
      *Given eternal life.

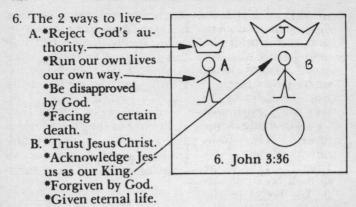

6. John 3:36

Which of these best represents the way you want to live?

*   *   *

When the explanation is complete, the drawings will look like this:

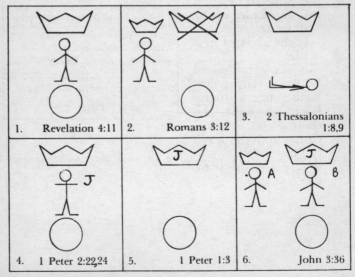

1. Revelation 4:11
2. Romans 3:12
3. 2 Thessalonians 1:8,9
4. 1 Peter 2:22,24
5. 1 Peter 1:3
6. John 3:36

You will notice that the reference to each verse has been written onto the drawing so that the person can look it up in a Bible for himself. They are also written in full, e.g. Revelation not Rev. This is important, as most people are unfamiliar with the Bible and especially abbreviations. The contents page of each Bible has the names of the books in full.

We encourage people to do the drawings as they speak. It requires a little skill, but has the advantage of emphasising each point as the picture is built up. At any time, e.g. as point six is being explained, it is easy to refer again to any of the previous points if necessary.

How to learn the outline
If you are teaching yourself to use this outline, it will help if you follow this procedure:
(a) Start learning from the Bible the verses which accompany each point.
(b) Learn the outline point by point and practise the drawings for each one.
(c) Practise the outline with someone else and continue to do so until you can present it with ease.
(d) Prepare some illustrations for points one to five.
(e) Plan your replies to responses one to four below.

The person to whom you are presenting this outline of the gospel will answer the final question, "Which of these represents the way you want to live?" in one of the following ways:
1. I wish to stay A.
2. I would like to be B but I am A.
3. I would like to be B but I am half-way between A and B.
4. I am B now.

Training others
If you use this outline to train others it can be done over a period of six to eight weeks taking one hour each week.

Follow the steps above but allow two weeks to practise step (e). Our previous experience has shown that people need more time to practise their replies to the alternative responses than for any other part of the outline.

IV WHAT TO SAY WHEN...

Often people are inhibited about trying to evangelise in case that they will be asked questions for which they don't have the answers. Some of us have actually been in that situation and have been strongly tempted to withdraw from trying again. Some don't even think about the possibility until the 'bomb' explodes!!

What questions?
Since our Department of Evangelism commenced Dialogue Evangelism home meetings, we have kept a list of the questions people asked. From a survey of five hundred meetings, the following questions were asked almost every time:

How do you know God exists?
Can you trust the New Testament documents?
Why does God allow suffering?
What happens to those who have never heard the gospel?
What about other religions?
Aren't all good people Christian?
Do you have to go to church to be a Christian?
Isn't faith only psychological?
Hasn't science disproved Christianity?

As these questions are asked so often we use them as a basis of a training programme in apologetics.

A training course?
Because these questions are asked so frequently, it would be helpful if ministers preached on them from time to

time. Such sermons have the double value of helping Christians to know how to answer as well as providing an opportunity to invite friends who have asked such questions to hear a Christian answer. These sermons will need to be supplemented with training programmes where people not only learn some answers but can practise giving them.

In the early stages of our training programmes we gave a series of addresses outlining possible answers. At the time people expressed appreciation, but we discovered that in a real life situation they were unable to recall or repeat the answers. We had given them answers, but no exercise in framing or giving these answers. Because of this we have now reversed the method.

At an introductory meeting we give the group a list of the questions commonly asked and we add any others which they have been asked. We select a question and make it the subject for our next meeting. Members of the group are asked to prepare an answer for that meeting and to be ready to try and convince us of the rightness of that answer. A list of books is provided to help the members in their preparation. When we meet again the answers are given in role-play situations where one takes the role of a sceptic and the others give their answers. The answers are evaluated at the end of the evening. People are encouraged to evaluate their own answers. We have noticed that in the role-play situation where people 'hear' their own answers they are often able to detect weaknesses which they had not noticed before.

This training method takes longer than the lecture method but we have been encouraged to continue using it because now our members are in fact able to give reasonable answers.

If video-taping is available to the group it is an added advantage. Tape the role-play and use it for reference when the evaluation session takes place.

If no training course is available to you then don't worry, train yourself! Most of our leaders did that anyway. Start reading the books in the list at the end of this section and formulate answers to the questions. Practise them on some of your friends.

However, before you encourage other people to prepare answers to the questions, you should discuss with them the principles to be followed when framing an answer. Then the best evangelistic use can be made of the question. What are these principles?

Principles which govern answers

Before answering a question, ask these 'questions' of your answer.

1.   Does it bring glory to God?
2.   Does it lead to the gospel?
3.   Does it answer the question behind the question?
4.   Is the answer believable?

1. Does it bring glory to God? This is the first of all questions to be asked. Is my answer one which will bring honour to God? Obviously it will have to be truthful. Have you noticed when people make a defence for Christianity they often exaggerate until that which is given is barely the truth. I have observed people giving testimony as to how they were converted. The black is painted blacker and the white, whiter until the story is no longer real and is quite unbelievable.

When answering a person's question the first principle to follow is that of *truthfulness*. Jesus says, "...I am the truth" (John 14:6), the Apostle Paul urges us to stop lying and tell the truth (Ephesians 4:25). We will never impress men and women that God's way is the way of truth if the method we use is untruthful. The truth is very appealing to people (and often quite novel). I remember on one occasion squirming as a man answered questions about the reliability of the New Testament documents—

"You don't have any information about Jesus outside the Bible do you?" his questioner asked.

"Plenty!"

"Like what?"

"Josephus the Jewish Historian tells about Jesus."

"But does he give any details about Jesus?"

"Josephus tells us about His miracles and His resurrection."

"About His resurrection?"

"Yes."

This is in fact true. But what he failed to say was that there is some controversy over those parts of Josephus' *History of the Jewish War* which refer to the resurrection, and some believe them to be Christian interpolations, as is the reference in Josephus' *Antiquities*.

Now the questioner may know nothing about the contents of the works of Josephus. But what if he does? Where are we then? Completely behind the eight ball! He will say, "He is too sweeping in the generalisations he draws from Josephus, he probably does the same with Jesus". Credibility will be lost and indeed should be. He would have helped the cause more by telling the truth. He could have said, "I read somewhere that the Jewish historian, Josephus, mentions Jesus but I really don't know much about his works".

God is not glorified in us when we act in a way which is unlike God's character. It is far better to say "I don't know" than to try to walk through the quicksands of half-truths. No one expects us to know everything—not even about Christianity. If they do they will soon be corrected.

The second principle to follow, if the answer is to be God honouring is *it will be loving*. The content and the method of the answer will be directed to the welfare of the questioner. The answer is not designed to show how clever I am but that another might know eternal life. Most of us find it difficult to admit we are wrong. Very few have ever done so publicly. Don't try to drive the person to whom you are speaking into an admission of error. Try introducing the answer with phrases like, "Have you ever considered that..." or "I hadn't ever given this much thought until some one pointed out to me that...and then I realised it really was worth thinking about". We are trying to make listening as easy as possible.

2. *Does it lead to the gospel?* The second question to ask about our answer is, "Will this answer lead the discussion towards the gospel or away from it?". All apologetics should be with a view that the person to whom we are speaking will become a Christian. It is

evangelistic. That is the whole reason for making a defence for Christianity.

Suppose you are asked "How do you know God exists?". This is a common question which every person is asked sooner or later. There are several possible answers which we could give, all of which are true.

We could argue from the creation around us. We could argue the existence of God from morality or conscience. It could be discussed from the person of Jesus Christ the man of history, or even from our own experience. Any of these answers could meet the principle we have stated, *Does it honour God?*, yet they may not necessarily lead us towards the gospel.

Let us examine some of the arguments we might use.

Arguing God's existence from creation can easily go wrong as in the following examples:

Case A

Q. Why do you believe God is there?

A. The wonderful world around us speaks of a creator.

Q. If God made the world, why didn't He do it properly?

A. What do you mean?

Q. Well earthquakes, tidal waves, children born deformed. Why did He do it like that?

Case B

Q. Why do you believe God is there?

A. The wonderful world around us speaks of a creator.

Q. Do you believe that stuff in the Bible about God making the world in seven days? Science has proved that isn't true!

To answer the questions about God's existence from the evidence of the world around us, invites the discussion to move in the direction of the problem of evil versus good or of science versus the Bible.

Using our own experience as evidence for God's existence is also likely to lead up a blind alley:

Case A

Q. Why do you believe God exists?

A. Because I have had an experience of Him.

Q. Do you feel Him? Can you see Him?

A. No, not really. I know I've been forgiven and I know

He is with me. I experience Jesus' life within me by the changed life He has brought me.

Q. Don't you think that's just a psychological way you have to cope with your inferiority and guilt? Plenty of people have experienced permanent changes in their lives and they aren't religious.

Case B

Q. Why do you believe God exists?

A. Because I have a personal experience of Him.

Q. Really! The woman who lives next door to me was telling me that she has had an experience of God, too.

A. Does she go to church anywhere?

Q. No, I think she is a Buddhist.

If we use the evidence of our experience to show the existence of God, the discussion will probably move in the direction of either comparative religions (and which one is the right one), or whether faith isn't just psychological.

Proving God on the evidence of conscience and morality will probably proceed like this:

Q. Do you believe in God's existence?

A. Yes, I believe God must exist because we all believe in right and wrong.

Q. What has right and wrong to do with God?

A. How do you know that something is wrong?

Q. I just do! My conscience tells me.

A. But conscience can be modified and conditioned to circumstances.

Q. I don't know whether anything is right or wrong in the way you say it is. I don't think that anything is right for all people for all times. I know what is right for me, it may be different for you. That's your business.

A. But what about when you and I meet? Would it be all right for me to kick your head in if I felt like it?

Q. Of course not!

A. But why not if I felt like it? Why couldn't I say, "I think it is O.K. for me to act like that"? You say that kind of behaviour is wrong, but I say it is right. How will we find out who is right? In the end only God can say what is right. When we don't believe in God we find it difficult to know on what basis to decide between what one person says is right and what another may say.

Q. I still don't believe in absolute right and wrong like that.

A. Your statement is an absolute statement. Where did you get it from? Did you make it up? Aren't you playing at being God? How will we check to see if your statement is accurate?

The argument on the basis of morality and conscience usually moves towards the area of absolute truth versus relative truth.

The evidence of the historical Jesus leads to the source of our knowledge of God—the Bible.

Q. Do you believe in God?

A. Yes I do, because of Jesus Christ.

Q. What does Jesus have to do with it?

A. This man lived in Palestine about 2,000 years ago. He claimed to be the Son of God in a unique way. I am convinced that His claim is established beyond reasonable doubt.

Q. How?

A. He made extraordinary claims, lived a life which seems to have been consistent with those claims. He predicted His death and resurrection and both happened exactly the way He said they would.

Q. Does that make Him God, though?

A. Not necessarily, but we aren't left many options. Such are His claims that if He isn't the Son of God, something is very wrong. He is either so badly mistaken as to be mad, or such a liar as to be evil. There is only one way for you to investigate for yourself. Have you read a history about Jesus?

Q. I went to Sunday School when I was young.

A. Why don't you select one of the four Gospels, either Matthew, Mark, Luke or John and read a biography of Jesus? As you do, ask yourself if the claim of Jesus to be the Son of God is well founded.

Q. But are those Gospels accurate histories? They were all written by people who were biased, weren't they?

This argument will invariably move towards the historicity of the New Testament documents and their reliability. When that is established, the person is directed to the Gospels to read for himself. This line of reasoning takes us straight to *the gospel*.

I am not saying that such lines of discussion are not true and valid. I use them all, but I will always favour the one which leads towards the gospel rather than away from it.

In all of the above cases, if the person concedes the possibility of God's existence, the most obvious question to follow should focus on the character of God and that should take us back to Jesus and the Gospels.

Our aim is not only to answer people's questions but to do it in such a way that they will consider the gospel and become Christians themselves.

3. Does it answer the question behind the question? The third question to ask when giving an answer is "Does this really answer the question which was asked?". Some books on evangelism suggest that it is a waste of time answering people's questions because only those who have the Holy Spirit can ever understand spiritual truths, and therefore we should answer each question with a re-statement of the gospel, since no question is ever a true question. As only the gospel can bring people to faith, to spend time answering questions will give us a false sense of our own ability.

I am opposed to that method of dealing with people and their questions. It is always difficult to know how far the 'image' of God in man has been marred. However, if a person can frame a question, he should be treated as a person and be given an answer.

There is an important limitation to be noted in apologetics. People are not converted by our answers to their questions; they are converted only through the gospel (Romans 1:16). However, the truthful, loving answering of questions can make the person able to listen to the gospel. Apologetics on one hand is the art of showing people that their 'hiding place' is not good enough and on the other that Christianity is not irrational.

Serious questions should be treated seriously. Sometimes we may suspect that there is a question behind the question. In that case, we should select an answer to meet that as well. When a person asks a question about the ultimate state of someone who has never heard about Jesus, he is asking for more than a doctrinal explanation. He may be saying "If those who have never heard about Jesus go to hell then the whole show is completely unjust", or "If they can get to heaven by some other method than by faith in Christ, then so can I!". With this in mind I can answer this way:

"I'm not actually sure what will happen to those who haven't heard about Jesus, but I am sure that God will act rightly. He never does anything that is unjust. However, what really worries me are those who have heard and have rejected. We aren't in any doubt what will happen to them."

On the question of suffering, I have noticed that people try to phrase the question in a fairly academic way like, "Why does God allow innocent children to suffer?" What he doesn't say is, "My child died last week and the doctors don't even know why. Why him and why us?" Whenever I answer the first question I use some phrase like "Christians believe the world is completely mucked up and some of us get more of the 'rough end' than others." If I'm told about some tragedy I seek to sympathise with the person. If I have had a similar experience, I say "I guess that must feel like...". If I haven't experienced such an event I say, "That must have been terrible I cannot imagine what that was like...".

When a person says "You cannot prove God exists, can you?". I always answer, "Yes, I can give you as much evidence for God's existence as we have for most things which we know are real".

Since none of us is a mind reader, we will not be able to know for sure whether there is a 'question' behind the question. If you can see the hidden question and if it is possible to answer both, then use an answer which covers both. If not, then answer truthfully the question asked and then enquire, "May I ask why that question is of interest to you?"

4. Is the answer believable? The last question to be

asked when framing an answer is "Will this answer be believed by the person?" Wherever possible we should avoid advancing an answer which we know is totally unacceptable because of previously stated views. This may not always be possible. If it is we should frame the answer in the most acceptable way, remembering that the truth must be told and done so lovingly. Sometimes the only answer which can be given will be totally unacceptable, and in that case because it is true, it will have to be given. This principle is the least important of all because often it cannot be applied, but where it can, it should be followed.

To summarise, when framing an answer ask yourself:

1. *Does it bring glory to God?*
2. *Does it lead to the gospel?*
3. *Does it answer the question behind the question?*
4. *Is the answer believable?*

In the training programme as people give their prepared answers to questions, the group should be encouraged to assess them using those four principles.

Answer with a question

As well as helping people prepare answers to questions which are likely to be asked, we need to point out the value of answering questions with a question. It may be possible to say "What do you think?" or "Would you like to elaborate on that question?" There are several advantages in doing this. It will help us to listen carefully to the other person. Often we are so busy thinking up our answers that we don't really hear what is said. It will also help us to discover the real question which is being asked, and will help the person speaking to us to clarify his thoughts. Sometimes people ask questions so that they can speak. They are not really interested in an answer. Asking them a question allows them to do this whereas if we just start straight in with our answer, they only become frustrated. To ask a question will help to keep the conversation alive and it means that we are not always placed in a defensive position. To ask a question will help the other person think out the reasons for his points of view. The question from us will also show that we don't believe we know everything. However, if a question is asked we should listen carefully and treat the answer seriously. Questions should not be asked to cover up our ignorance or just to give more time for us to think out our answers.

A reading list
The following are some of the books which we suggest people read to assist in the preparation of their answers.

Know What You Believe. Paul Little. (Scripture Union)
How to Give Away Your Faith. Paul Little, (IVP)
Basic Christianity. John R.W. Stott, (IVP)
Christianity and Comparative Religion. J.N.D. Anderson, (IVP)
Escape From Reason. Francis A. Schaeffer, (IVP)
Runaway World. Michael Green, (IVP)
What is Human? T.M. Kitwood, (IVP)
The Books and the Parchments. F.F. Bruce, (IVP)
The New Testament Documents, Are They Reliable? F.F. Bruce, (Pickering & Inglis)
Is Anybody There? David C.K. Watson, (Hodder & Stoughton)
Knowing God. James Packer, (Hodder & Stoughton)
The Man and the Book. John C. Chapman, (AIO Sydney)
Evidence that Demands a Verdict. Josh. McDowell, (Here's Life Publishers)

What needs to be done?
In training ourselves or others for evangelism, we have examined the value of the godly life, the importance of having at our fingertips a gospel so well known that we can give our attention to people, to listen carefully to them, and not have to rack our brains to know what to say. We have discussed the importance of having well thought out answers to the questions which are usually asked, and the thing we have to do now is find some way to put our knowledge into action.

V PRINCIPLES INVOLVED WHEN CHOOSING A METHOD

It is very important at this stage in the training programme to find a method which we can use with the gifts we have, given the opportunities which come our way. Before we look at some available methods, we ought to think how we can assess the value of one method against another so that we will choose wisely and know when to change our methods. Some methods may work in one situation and not in another. Is it possible to know beforehand if it is a good method for us to use in our situation?

What governs my choice?

I remember how painful it was several years ago to read the opening chapter of Gavin Reid's book *The Gagging of God*. He described a parish mission in a local church. A group of students from a theological college had come to help. Good preparations had been made, yet no real 'outsiders' had been contacted. A painful chapter to read because it reminded me of several parish missions with which I had been associated, where the congregation on Wednesday night was identical to that on any Sunday morning. We had in fact reached out to no one. We had high hopes. Someone remembered in the past that outsiders had come. Yet at that time this was not happening. It was *not* a good evangelistic method for that time. It had been in the past, it was *not* at the moment. We should stop using such methods because they create for us the illusion that we are achieving something when in fact we are doing no real evangelism at all, and when that is the case, it is important to know it and say so. What does constitute a good evangelistic method?

1. Are unbelievers present? Whether it is a home meeting, a personal conversation, an open air meeting or a large crusade, the first question to ask is whether unbelievers and 'outsiders' will, in fact, be present. In this matter we need to be quite ruthless with ourselves. Let's be done with the 'someone-might-walk-in-off-the-street' idea. If the method we are using doesn't reach out to unbelievers, what we are doing is not evangelism. It will help the Christians and be a blessing to them to hear the gospel but we are misled if we think evangelism is actually taking place.

Often we are not really sure if outsiders will come and we will have to make an informed guess. Most people will be able to tell you beforehand if this is the kind of gathering to which they will be happy to bring their uncommitted friends.

We originally began the series of home meetings called Dialogue Evangelism because we simply could not get unbelievers to come to Guest Services at our church. However ten years later we were able to get people to come to church and so the Guest Service became an effective method again. We were in a new social and spiritual climate. In the late 1960's, the Guest Service only gave the *illusion* of evangelism. In the early 1980's, it was *real* evangelism.

It should be noted that the effectiveness of all evangelistic methods changes from time to time, place to place, and person to person. What works in one place may not work in another. What does not work at one time is often tailor-made for a new situation. One person may use a method which another never can. However, the first question always is "Are there unbelievers present?" If not, the method is wrong.

2. *Is the gospel truly preached?* It is possible to have outsiders present at a large or small gathering, and for evangelism not to take place because the gospel was not truly preached. But this can really only happen through carelessness. Either the carelessness of the organisers or the carelessness of the evangelist. It is the responsibility of the organiser to see, not only that unbelievers are present but that the gospel is preached.

It may seem strange that this point should be laboured, but often too little time is given to the most crucial of all arrangements. Evangelists should be chosen primarily because they regularly, indeed repeatedly, tell the gospel in a way which is true to the Scriptures and which can be understood by the hearer. It is important that he is a good communicator but it is essential that whatever else happens he 'delivers the goods'.

I heard of a meeting of ministers who had been called together to discuss the possibility of holding an evangelistic crusade in their area. A group of them was anxious to invite an up-and-coming young evangelist who had worked in other areas of their city. These men had come with a movie showing the large crowds which were turning up to hear the evangelist, and also the large numbers of people responding to the preaching and coming forward for counselling. Statistics were quoted to establish these as facts and to show that the film was not an exaggeration. One of the ministers asked if there were tapes available of his sermons because he would like to be assured that the gospel was being preached. Unfortunately tapes were not available, and the promoters seemed to think that the request was unreasonable in the light of the large numbers of people who were seen to be making decisions!

It seemed to me not only a very reasonable request but an absolutely necessary one if a true assessment of that evangelistic project was to be made. If the gospel is not preached, then evangelism is not taking place. The number of people who respond is not the test that the gospel is preached.

Often in personal evangelism we stop short of telling people the gospel for fear of losing their friendship. For years I worked on a Beach Mission team where we talked about 'building bridges of friendship' as a prerequisite for evangelism, and I think that is right. But I fear we spent so much time building bridges, we never had any time left to cross them. Potentially good opportunities were lost because no gospel was preached!

In addition to the questions *Are there unbelievers present?*, and *Is the gospel truly preached?*, the next question to ask is *Can the preacher be understood?*

3. Can the preacher be understood? It may seem obvious to ask whether the gospel is truly preached. However, it does not always seem so obvious to ask whether that gospel is presented in meaningful ways. So often even the words are misunderstood or not understood at all. I regularly drive past a church building on my way to work. It is built on a corner where traffic lights change regularly. It is an ideal site for an evangelistic sign since cars are usually held up every few minutes by the lights. For months the large notice board was used to advertise a Day Nursery run by the church—not altogether a clear gospel message! However a month before Easter a notice went up. It was well done in bold lettering. It read "DEATH IS SWALLOWED UP IN VICTORY". Let's test this piece of evangelism by the criteria I've suggested. Are there unbelievers present? Hundreds, maybe even thousands, daily! Is the gospel truly preached? Yes! Can it be understood? No way!!

That statement is a 'shorthand' way of reminding the Christian of everything good in the Christian life. It recalls how Jesus died and rose so our sins could be forgiven. It reminds us that the punishment of our sins has been taken in the death of Jesus. I recall how death has no terrors for me now I am in Christ. It tells me how death is swallowed up in the victory of Christ.

But what does it say to the uninitiated? He can work out how a victory could be swallowed up in death. He will be mystified about the reverse. He will say to himself, "If I went to that church, there is no way I would understand them. I can't even understand the notice they put up for me to read". He concludes he will never make it, so he rejects it as a possibility. In every way that sign had the makings of a superb piece of evangelism but more care needed to be taken on the wording of the message.

Originally there were plenty of unbelievers but no gospel (only a Day Nursery advertisement). Then there were both unbelievers and the gospel, but it was expressed in a way which couldn't be understood. Even something simple like 'God exists and cares about you' would have been better. As I have already pointed out, our problem at present is, that technical words like *sin, repentance, justification, saved, hell, judgment,* etc., are in common English usage, but generally no longer mean what the Bible means when using them.

There is a story told about a computer which translated from English to Russian. The message was fed in, and it typed back the Russian equivalent. An experimental message "The spirit is willing but the flesh is indeed weak" was fed in and out came the Russian equivalent. To check the accuracy the Russian text was re-fed and it typed back "The steak is not good but the vodka is excellent"!

The two gospel outlines suggested in Part III of this chapter, have been put together so that people will be able to understand the gospel clearly.

I remember once at a Beach Mission trying to explain the gospel to a young man. I thought I was making good headway, when suddenly he said, "I can't understand what you are talking about!"

"Don't give up on me, let me try again," I said. So I did. He said it was slightly clearer and invited me to try yet again. It was a painful exercise for me as we walked up and down the beach. I made several attempts to find alternative words and phrases for those well known 'jargon words' which had taken over my religious vocabulary. The most painful part about the whole exercise was to discover that I really didn't know what I meant by most of them. I had never taken the trouble to sharpen up my ideas so that the gospel was so clear to me that I was able to explain it *clearly* to another.

I don't for a moment suggest that this exercise of finding meaningful equivalents is easy, but I do suggest that it is necessary. It is the responsibility of all evangelists, both professional and part-timers, to work so that the gospel is clearly understood.

The last question to ask of a possible method is "Will a person be able to listen *with ease* if I tell him the gospel this way?".

4. Does the atmosphere encourage listening? It is possible to organise an evangelistic project which has unbelievers present, and where the gospel is well preached in terms readily understood, and for the exercise to be less than helpful. This often happens because the 'atmosphere' of the gathering makes it difficult to hear the message. It could be a coffee shop where the music is continuous and so loud that conversation is made virtually impossible, yet I have spoken at coffee shops where the atmosphere was great and helpful to both speaker and listener. Sometimes people have been invited to meetings in homes without being told that someone would speak or indeed that anything religious would take place. An otherwise good evangelistic church service is ruined because so much time is taken up before the sermon with singing and items, so that everyone is too weary to listen to the gospel when it is preached. In a personal conversation, we need to be sensitive enough to stop when the person does not want us to speak any more.

Sometimes a less than friendly attitude makes it hard for people to hear what is said. A friend of mine tells how as a young man he moved from one State to another to work. He went to church on Sunday night. The minister said to him "You come from *there*? Well, we are evangelicals *here*!"

My friend said to me "I had never heard the word 'evangelical' used before, but I knew he had been rude!"

When we are planning we should ask "What can be done to make listening to the gospel easier?" If we organise ourselves so that hearing the gospel is made difficult, we have no one else to blame but ourselves.

Every evangelistic method and technique needs to be constantly reviewed because its effectiveness may change with time. Remember to ask yourself:

1.   *Are there unbelievers present?*
2.   *Is the gospel faithfully presented?*
3.   *Can people understand what is being said?*
4.   *Does the atmosphere help people to listen?*

When you have four affirmatives, whatever you are doing, whether it is one-to-one evangelism, or a large public gathering, then it's 'all systems go'!

VI   FINDING A METHOD FOR YOU

The first training course in evangelism in which I took part lasted half an hour. A group of us met one Sunday afternoon at the church. The minister gave each of us a packet of material containing some publicity about the church, a gospel and a small tract. We were paired off and allocated a number of houses to visit in our suburb. We prayed together, (and how I prayed), and off we went.

I had been converted for some years, and I think I could have made a fair attempt at explaining the gospel, although I wasn't able to do so in any thought-out way. There are few exercises which I have ever undertaken for which I was so ill equipped!

As an evangelistic effort, the afternoon was of course a disaster, but I decided then that I would never again embark on evangelism without either training myself or being trained by someone else, nor would I ask anyone else to do so.

I have observed over many years that every now and again churches take up some new evangelistic activity with such zeal that it takes up all their time and energy. It might be a visitation programme or a series of home meetings.

Every church member is urged to participate, and it is presented to them as a matter of Christian obedience. Status within the church depends upon commitment to the programme. Some Christians take to the programme like ducks to water, it seems to be tailor-made for them. Others do it out of a sense of loyalty to the church programme but don't really enjoy it, and others just cannot work the model being offered at all. These latter ones will drop out of the programme, they may or may not give a reason for doing so, but they will undoubtedly feel guilty and may be made to feel as if their discipleship is in question.

After a few years the church may swing into a new programme with the same zeal with which they began the former one. Some 'drop-outs' may be picked up in the new programme but others will bow out.

Because of this I am convinced that in any programme there should be a choice of methods offered to people, but there should also be variations within the methods. The last part of any training programme will be to encourage 'trainees' to consider which of the available methods they would like to train for.

I have already stated that all Christians should seek to evangelise and that all should be able to articulate the gospel. Consequently the training I have already spoken about will be general training for all Christians. Specific training in specialised methods will come last. This variety cannot be achieved overnight nor can all be implemented at once. What I am suggesting is that training in the use of a particular method be selective rather than general, and that when one programme is underway successfully, another can be started to cater for other people. Each programme should develop its own trainers who can do on the job training, and should have its own fellowshipping groups to encourage the members to continue with the programme. From time to time the congregation will hear about the work, and will pray about the programme.

The following is a list of some of the models I have observed working, together with some variations within each model.

Door-to-door visiting

1. Pairs of Christians have visited every house in the street. The approach has been direct 'My name is...we come from St Aidan's Church—the one on the hill. We've come to ask if we can talk to you about Jesus Christ'.

2. Some found they couldn't do that. The constant refusal was too hard to handle so they visited the night before and left a card in the box. It read:

'Dear Householder,
My name is...I come from St Aidan's Church and tomorrow night I'm planning to visit people in this street to tell you about our church'.

This method screened out several people who were 'not in' or at least didn't answer the door.

3. Others varied the method by giving away a Gospel. Their approach went like this—'My name, etc...We are visiting the houses in the area to give people a copy of a modern translation of Mark's Gospel. We don't know if you have seen it. We've been impressed by it and would like you to have one'.

Another variation on this approach was—'We meet at John Brown's home in this street, number forty-seven, on Tuesday nights to read and talk about this Gospel. The Browns' phone number is on the back page—you could phone them or just come along at 7.30 on Tuesday night'.
4.   Some people found that even this way was too difficult to begin with and they took part in a series of letter-box drops. These advertised a free correspondence course in 'Understanding Christianity', or included a seasonal message (Easter, Christmas, etc.), gave details about the church services, and a list of the sermon topics for the next month/quarter.

The door-to-door visiting team discovered people who were in need of specialised visits. Some were in material need, others were old and shut in. This provided work for a new model altogether, that of specific house visiting.

Specific house visiting
1.   The elderly and shut in people were visited by some members who did not wish to take part in the door-to-door visiting. Again the visit varied with the person. Some ladies baked a cake and went to tea. Some spoke about church and played a tape of Sunday's sermon or of a shorter talk which had been specially done for these visits. These tapes were made by other Christians who were not necessarily members of the visiting team. Some just talked and where possible, said something Christian. Others were able to show a film strip. The trainer of this method had worked with her team until they found a way which suited each member.
2.   Another group visited the parents of children who were associated with the church through Sunday School and clubs. Their approach was 'We'd like to come and visit you and talk about Sarah's progress at Sunday School, and to put you in the picture about what we hope will happen this term'.
3.   The *Evangelism Explosion* method has been used

with much success in many churches. It offers another alternative model for home visiting. It is documented in the book *Evangelism Explosion* by D. James Kennedy.

4.   I heard a man tell that he was converted by reading *The Good News Bible*. He said that someone had left it in his home but no one could even remember who. He said, "I started to read it and had read Matthew, Mark and was nearly finished Luke when I realised Jesus was the Son of God and I wasn't relating to Him properly. I knelt down and said, 'I don't really know what to say, but whatever I'm supposed to say I want to say it'." He looked in the phone book for a church in his area and rang the minister to tell him. He was visited and linked into the ongoing life of that congregation.

He said, "I didn't know anyone else who was converted like that but I couldn't see why it shouldn't happen again. So my wife and I go around on Saturday afternoon with a few copies of 'The Good News Bible' and sell them. I simply say, 'This is a modern translation of the New Testament which I am selling. It costs "£x" and is a very good buy'. We never fail to get into worthwhile conversations. You don't need many evangelistic skills to do that." You need plenty of another commodity however!!

He found a method which he could use and continue indefinitely.

Using your home for evangelism

Again the models will vary with the people.

1.   Dialogue evangelism is done by inviting non-church going friends home to discuss Christianity. The approach goes like this, 'Jean and I are having a few friends to meet our friend, Bill Bloggs and to discuss Christianity with him. He'll give a short talk and then we will be able to spend the rest of the evening asking questions and discussing them. By the way, it's for dinner'. A small team is involved. The host and hostess bring the guests (by far the hardest work), the dialogue leader gives a talk and answers questions. The skills required by each one are quite different.

2.   An interesting variation on the above method can be done seasonally, say at Christmas or Easter.

Several years ago I met a man who told me he always held his Christmas party for his working colleagues on the Sunday evening before Christmas. He invited his guests to come to the Carol Service at his church beforehand. This service was always evangelistic, but because it was Christmas, most of his non-christian friends came along. The party/carol service has become an institution.

3.   Sometimes opportunities occur very suddenly, such as when some social or moral issue arises, and especially when the media provide both the interest and publicity, e.g. abortion, euthanasia, etc.

Invitations would be issued like this, 'Joan and I are having a few friends around to meet a friend of ours, Dr Bill Bloggs, and to discuss the Christian view on (whatever), would you and Mary like to come?'.

4.   I have learned of a church which has an outreach called *Christianity Explained*. A team drops into about two hundred homes a brochure advertising the six week *Christianity Explained* course to be held in a designated home in the area. A few days later the team members visit the homes and recruit people to join this course. They told me that they were enrolling about five persons from every two hundred homes. The course is evangelistic and is designed around Mark's Gospel which they read during the six weeks of the study course. The team required to do this includes the group of visitors and two persons able to teach the course.

The members of the team have done some research into the average length of time people lived in the area and discovered it to be about seven years. They have divided their suburb into areas for visiting (two hundred homes at a time) and plan to visit the whole suburb over the next seven years. By then they will be able to begin the cycle of visitation and recruitment again.

5.   I observed an interesting piece of evangelism when I was associated with the University of New England in New South Wales. It is a residential university. A young Christian man invited his friends, two at a time, to read through a Gospel with them. His approach was quite

direct 'Have you ever read about Jesus? What about meeting with me after tea on Wednesdays for an hour and we'll read through a Gospel. What do you have to lose?' At one stage he was reading with different people on five evenings of the week.

Evangelism at church

We are all familiar with evangelistic meetings and services held at church. Care needs to be taken when using this method not to engage in 'in group' activities. When selecting hymns the non-church-goer is the one to consider. Will he know it? Will the members be able to sing it well enough for others to learn it easily?

I have noticed that when the evangelistic service becomes an institution, the church members treat it like any other service. They fail to pray about it and they fail to bring their friends. Although I believe the evangelistic service should be held on a regular basis, it should *appear* to be held on an *irregular* basis, and the members need to be carefully prepared for each one.

1.   They need to know and have confidence in the evangelist, whether he is their own minister or a visitor. If he is a visitor, it is desirable to have him preach in the church a few weeks before so the congregation can gain confidence to invite their non-christian friends.

2.   The members need to pray for the evangelist and also for the people they are going to invite. It has been found helpful to have cards printed for members to make a commitment to pray.

3.   They need to be encouraged to attend the service whether they were able to get someone to come with them or not. Often people work hard at inviting their friends. When their invitation is refused they are disappointed, often feel guilty and would rather not be seen 'empty handed' at the service. They specially need encouragement and that needs to be given beforehand.

Members need to be taught that they exercise a ministry simply by attending. They will be able to be friendly to new people who have come. They will be free to take over jobs which always need to be done and to free people who have guests so they can be with them. They should be encouraged to speak to people before and after the service. It is imperative that they do not stay away.

For several years we have run lunch time Bible studies for business people in the city. From time to time we have an evangelistic meeting. We urge members to bring their friends. We find, to our consternation, that when they are unsuccessful in being able to do this, they stay away. The attendance is smaller by half. We are all disappointed and the outsiders who come along are given a falsely adverse impression of the group.

4.   Members need to be encouraged to plan the best way to entertain their friends afterwards so that they can engage in some follow-up ministry. Encourage them to think out whether they will take their visitors home for a meal (or coffee, depending on the time) or whether they will stay for coffee in the church hall. In some churches people are genuinely friendly and will come and introduce themselves to visitors. We need to weigh that advantage against the disadvantage that while they do that, we will not talk about the gospel we have just heard. I have found it more successful to invite my friends for a meal before we go to an evening service. When they say they will come, I say "Can you make it for dinner/tea before?" I have fewer last minute refusals.

We all need to be alert in our conversation to be ready to follow-up the message or sermon. For years I always asked my friends, "What did you think of that?"

They invariably said, "Quite good". I also thought it was good and conversation moved onto the weather or the football. My latest try has been more successful, I note the part of the sermon which is right at the heart of the gospel and say, "I thought the point he made about the death of Jesus for the forgiveness of our sins was very powerful".

To have a training day where these matters can be raised will be helpful to the church members. It will also have the added advantage of demonstrating how important this evangelistic service is. It is not just another Sunday service.

What about the service?
Everything about the evangelistic service needs to be planned with the outsider in mind. The singing, the reading of the Bible and the prayers are to focus on, and help the preaching of, the gospel. Notices given should be applicable to the outsider. On one occasion I preached at an evangelistic service where the church treasurer gave a long and complicated explanation about how the church free-will giving envelope system worked. It couldn't have been done at a less appropriate time. It distracted us all from the gospel.

When singing groups are invited we need to stress to them how important it is for us to *hear* the words they are singing.

I have noticed that when people depart from their normal service and have a special service, whether they have liturgical services or not, the service generally takes much longer and the preaching is pushed back to the end of a long programme when people are least able to listen. Preaching is central in evangelism and everything should be geared to it.

A bookstall and tape library
Both the bookstall and the tape library can be used helpfully at the evangelistic service. When stocking the bookstall, a few well chosen evangelistic books rather than a wide range is preferable. The stranger generally does not know what he is looking for and becomes confused if there is a wide range. A brief, well prepared book review is helpful to direct people to specific needs.

To have the sermon tape available will mean that members are able to lend it to friends who were not at the service, and those who were there, are able to hear it again at their leisure.

A testimony?
To have people tell how and when they became Christians can be very helpful. It shows that people do listen to the gospel and respond to it. Try to have various

church members give testimony rather than special visiting 'greats'. The people who attend evangelistic services are usually friends of members and it can help to hear about people like themselves. This can be done by a person giving a short talk telling of the circumstance by which he came to hear and understand the gospel, how he responded to it and what difference this has made to his life. It is sometimes helpful to have two people with quite different backgrounds to speak, as it will show that God deals individually with different people.

Those giving the talks need to be reminded that their talk is to focus on what Jesus has done for them in their life rather than to preach. Honesty, as in all things, needs to be stressed so that the story is told 'as it is'.

For variation the person can be interviewed. This has several advantages. For people not skilled in giving talks it means they don't have to remember what they are going to say. The interviewer takes responsibility to get the testimony started and more importantly he takes responsibility for its conclusion. If the person being interviewed is not expressing himself clearly this can be dealt with by a question from the interviewer.

I have developed a pattern of questions in interviews by asking questions like these:

Did you grow up in a Christian home?
What makes you say that?
How did you come to understand the gospel?
What did you do to respond to the gospel?
What is the hardest part of the Christian life?
What is the best part of the Christian life?

Before the meeting I tell the person the questions I'm going to ask and we go over his responses, then we both know what is to happen.

One of the advantages of evangelism at church is that the members are able to observe their minister, or a visiting preacher, evangelising their friends and so they learn another method of evangelism. It is also a challenge to the members to continue their own work of evangelism. Because the meeting is special, it gives each member a new reason to broach the subject with the friend they invited. Irrespective of how many other evangelistic models are being used in a church, this one should not be neglected. Some people will be able to bring a friend who hasn't been able to work in any of the other schemes, and we are all stimulated to engage in our evangelistic work in other places simply because it is happening so naturally at church.

Conclusion

Let us imagine yours is a church where no real evangelism has taken place. It is decided to begin a training programme like one suggested in this book. By the time you read through this section on finding a method, the thought of having many schemes going simultaneously may be so overwhelming that you will be tempted to give up. Don't!

1.   Do not try to start everything at once.
2.   Find a method which you think will be useful for your district.
3.   Invite people to train specifically for it.
4.   Stay with that programme until leaders are trained, able to train others, and keep the programme going.
5.   Then select another method in which you have confidence, and begin training people for it.

The number of different methods will vary from church to church depending on the size of the congregation and the gifts of the members.

Don't be put off by the large variety of methods available. Starting somewhere is preferable to doing nothing!

VII NURTURING NEW CONVERTS

So far in our training programme we have dealt with the general witness of the 'trainee' through Christian living; we have taught him a gospel outline, given him some basic apologetics and found a method which he can use personally. There remains now to suggest the principles he needs to follow so that adequate nurture and care will be given to new converts.

They will need to be established in the Christian life,

integrated into a church, and will need to equip them-selves to lead people to Christ. This nurture should be done at two levels, personally by the one who leads him to Christ, and corporately by the church which he decides to attend.

Principles of Christian growth

The new Christian will look to the person who has led him to Christ to counsel him in the new life into which he has moved. Some basic instruction on the principles of Christian growth should be given when the person becomes a Christian. These should include:

1. *Study of the Bible*
2. *Praying*
3. *Fellowship with other Christians*
4. *Witnessing.*

1. Study of the Bible. The counsellor should enquire as to whether the convert has a Bible and whether it is in a modern translation. If he hasn't, the counsellor should give some advice about the type to buy. There are so many available that it can be difficult to make a choice, but in the meantime, he should be given a Gospel to begin reading.

The counsellor should share with the new Christian his own method of reading the Bible or if he feels that may be too complicated for a beginner, he should make some alternative suggestion. He needs to:—

(a) Show how important it is to read the Bible, because it is there that he will find what God is like and will be able to know how to please Him.

(b) Work out with the person a satisfactory time of the day when this could be done. He needs to be encouraged to do it regularly.

(c) Suggest where in the Bible to begin. I suggest reading through one of the Gospels, perhaps John or Mark, then the Acts of the Apostles, then Genesis.

(d) Give some suggestion as to how to do it. I would suggest he begins by praying that God will help him to understand and obey what he is reading. Then read the chapter or paragraph he has selected. Ask the question

'What does this part of the Bible tell me about God?'. Keep a note book and write down a brief note in answer to the question. Think about how he should act in the light of what he has discovered. Note it down. Pray about his decision.

It would be helpful if the counsellor could meet with the person as soon as possible and do this exercise with him.

2. *Praying.* Prayer is as important as regular Bible reading, and the new convert needs to be taught to pray. This should be done by reminding him that he has come into a new relationship with Christ who is a person, and who wishes to be spoken to like everyone else. Once again it will be helpful if the counsellor shares with the convert how he goes about his own praying. What is important in the early stages is that the new Christian is not over-whelmed by the suggested programme. I suggest something like this:—

'At the same time as I read the Bible I also pray. I speak quite naturally as I would to you. I know that Jesus is a friend and wishes me to speak with Him. I know He is God and so I will speak with reverence. I start by thanking God for the good things He has given me, then I go over the day in my thoughts and share with Him both the good things and the bad. For some I give thanks, for others I ask for forgiveness and strength. Then I pray for other people—members of my family, friends who don't know Christ, etc. I have made a list of them which I keep in my Bible so I won't forget them. Then I pray for myself. , .'

I stress again how important it is for the counsellor to meet and do this with the convert early in his new Christian life.

As part of the training of people in this aspect of evangelism the 'trainee' should be encouraged to examine his own devotional life. He will not be able to encourage the new Christian either with sympathy or with a realistic programme if he does not pray and read the Bible regularly himself. This needs to be stressed not only in initial training but also in refresher courses.

3. *Fellowship with other Christians.* This aspect of Christian growth will also need to be taught to the new Christian. His counsellor should make a time to meet regularly with him so they can share their Christian lives together. The new Christian should be encouraged to make a note of parts of the Bible which are obscure so that at these meetings he can ask for some light to be shown on them.

There are excellent study programmes available to assist counsellors and new Christians during these times, such as: *The Navigators' Programme*, the Billy Graham Association's *Seven Basic Bible Studies*, the Campus Crusade for Christ's material, and *The Touch of His Hand* by the World Home Bible League.

These programmes are designed so that each week both the counsellor and the new Christian answer questions from the Bible. These are recorded in a workbook or on a printed sheet, which can be compared and corrected. They also pray together as they meet. This method has the immediate advantages of both re-stating the gospel, and encouraging the new Christian to see that he has a responsibility to pray for and minister to other Christians, as well as receiving from them. If such a programme is not followed, it is essential when meeting with the new Christian to revise the gospel again with him. It is essential to ensure that his understanding of the gospel is clear and that his assurance of salvation rests only on the work of Christ and not on his own experience or his feelings.

The counsellor has a further responsibility to see the new Christian linked with a church. If the person is already a church-goer, the counsellor may not need to do much more than alert the minister about this new Christian. If the new Christian doesn't go to church, the counsellor should stress the importance of Christian fellowship and teaching, and work out with him the best church to attend. The new Christian may decide to join the church of his counsellor, or if that is impracticable, to join one elsewhere. Whatever decision is made, the counsellor should arrange to go *with* him to church until contact has been established with the other Christians there, and until he has learned to settle into that new environment.

As time goes by, the counsellor's aim is to integrate the new Christian into the life of the congregation so that the one-to-one Bible study/counselling gives way to the wider ministry of the local church. The counsellor then does not remain a 'guru' forever.

4. Witnessing. This final aspect of Christian growth should be included in the training programme so that when the 'trainee' becomes the counsellor, he will not neglect to help the new Christian to witness to his friends. Most new Christians have a desire to witness and should be encouraged to do so. The immediate advantage of having a gospel outline like the ones already suggested, is that the new Christian can be encouraged to share that outline with his friends. Whenever the new Christian is able, he too should train to do the work of evangelism, so that he in turn will become a soul-winner and a nurturer of others. This should be our aim for all converts in our care.

It all takes time
This nurturing of new Christians is always time consuming, and people involved in the training programme need to be aware of this so that they make extra time available for it in their weekly programme.

CHAPTER TWELVE

Power for Evangelism

'Power for Evangelism' is to help us see that there is available for each of us, all that we need to be obedient to God's call to share in His gospelling of the world. We need to avail ourselves of this power.

The Holy Spirit and the believer

Just before Jesus ascended into heaven He commanded His followers to wait in Jerusalem until they received the Holy Spirit. His coming would give them power for their new mission, "But you will receive power when the Holy Spirit comes upon you, and you will be my witnesses in Jerusalem, and in all Judea and Samaria, and to the ends of the earth" (Acts 1:8). There is no doubt that the coming of the Holy Spirit to the followers of Jesus transformed them from frightened men and women into bold witnesses to the fact that Jesus was alive and was indeed the unique Son of God.

The first disciples were unique

Just as the coming of Jesus into the world was quite unique, so was the experience of the first disciples. Many of them had been 'Old Testament' believers. They knew the promise of God that He would send His King into the world who would 'save His people from their sins'. They waited with eager expectation in the certainty that God would keep His promise. When Jesus came they recognised Him to be the fulfilment of their longing hope. They confessed Him to be the Messiah (Matthew

16:16). They saw in Him glory, "...the glory of the one and only Son, who came from the Father, full of grace and truth" (John 1:14). After Jesus' resurrection from the dead, Thomas confessed Him to be his Lord and God (John 20:28). Yet in spite of this, these men were not really Christians in the New Testament sense until the Holy Spirit came to them at Pentecost.

John in his Gospel makes this clear in the comment he makes on the statement of Jesus "If any man is thirsty, let him come to me and drink. Whoever believes in me, as the Scripture has said, streams of living water will flow from within him". John states "By this he meant the Spirit, whom those who believe in him were later to receive. Up to that time the Spirit had not been given, since Jesus had not yet been glorified" (John 7:37-39). *They* did not receive the Holy Spirit until Pentecost, although He (the Holy Spirit) is available now for all those who believe on Jesus.

This same idea is restated in Peter's comments after Cornelius received the Holy Spirit. "As I began to speak, the Holy Spirit came on them as he had come on us at the beginning...So if God gave them the same gift as he gave us, who believed in the Lord Jesus Christ, who was I to think that I could oppose God!" (Acts 11:15-17).

Two important phrases are noteworthy, Peter describes his experience at Pentecost as "at the beginning" (verse 15) and as a result of "believing in the Lord Jesus" (verse 17).

Their experience is not like ours. It was unique. Some had believed God's promise before Jesus was born. They had seen, heard and lived with Jesus (1 John 1:1). They had witnessed His death and resurrection. They saw Him ascend into heaven. They experienced the coming of the Holy Spirit at Pentecost. All of these were unique events, which we are only able to experience by reading about them in the Gospels and the Acts of the Apostles. These disciples stand in the unique position of being 'transitional', between the Old Testament believers and the New Testament believers none of whom ever saw or heard Jesus. Nor have we.

What we do have in common with them is the Holy

Spirit, who comes to all who believe in Jesus (John 7:37-39), and constantly ministers the things of Christ to us (John 14:26). He convinces us of sin and our need of forgiveness (John 16:8-11). He brings us to new birth (John 3:5), and changes us into Christ-like people (2 Corinthians 3:18), and in doing so gives us the love for God and the love for our fellow men which is the power for evangelism.

The power to engage in the work of evangelism which comes from the Holy Spirit is not magical. He causes us to love (Romans 5:5; Galations 5:22; 2 Corinthians 5:14,15). All believers have received the Holy Spirit (1 Corinthians 12:3), and we need to co-operate with Him and not to grieve Him or quench Him, as He creates in us love for God and love for our fellow men.

Love—a powerful force

Those who are loved respond by loving. God loves us, and His love was demonstrated chiefly in sending His Son to die for us (John 3:16). We do not cause God to love us. He does so because of His character. It is of the very essence of His person (1 John 4:16). Our love for God comes *as a response to His action*. When we contemplate how much God has loved us, how much we have been forgiven, and at what great cost to Jesus, we become more and more motivated to love God in return. True love for God will be demonstrated in obedience (John 14:15). Doing what Christ commands is the only real way we have to show how much we love Him.

Evangelism, as we have seen, is one of the ways in which we can obey Christ. We are in no doubt about Christ's desire that all should hear the gospel (Matthew 28:19). If we don't spend time meditating on God's love for us we will begin to take it for granted, our love for God will grow cold. We will find obedience a terrible drudgery instead of a grateful response. Love for God needs to be cultivated and practised. The motivation to love God comes from God's love to us, "This is love: not that we loved God, but that he loved us and sent his Son as an atoning sacrifice for our sins" (1 John 4:10).

The man who has been forgiven much, loves much (Luke 7:47). A right understanding of our real sinfulness and of our new position in Christ and the great inheritance which awaits us (1 John 3:1-3), will cause our love for God to increase. This love must issue, not in feelings, but in actions. Love is not how I feel but how I act. It needs to be stressed that time needs to be given by all Christians to meditate on what God has done for us in Christ. We need to pray that God's love which has been given to us (Romans 5:5), will grow more and more. We need to pray that our love for our fellow men will increase.

It was said of Jesus that when He looked on the crowds "he had compassion on them, because they were harassed and helpless, like sheep without a shepherd" (Matthew 9:36). Can I ask you how you react to the crowds around you, your friends and your neighbours? Do you have concern for them? The Apostle Paul said about his countrymen "...my heart's desire and prayer to God for the Israelites is that they may be saved" (Romans 10:1). He said he had great sorrow and increasing anguish in his heart about them (Romans 9:2). I cannot read these passages without feeling a sense of guilt for my own hardness of heart.

To grow like Jesus is to love people and to seek ways to bring the gospel to them.

Prayer—a powerful agency

When the Apostle James encourages us to continue praying, he reminds us of the power of prayer. "...The prayer of a righteous man is powerful and effective. Elijah was a man just like us. He prayed earnestly that it would not rain, and it did not rain on the land for three and a half years. Again he prayed, and the heavens gave rain, and the earth produced its crops" (James 5:16-18). That is very powerful praying whichever way we look at it! Prayer works. God longs to hear and answer our prayers. He will certainly do so.

Evangelism, like swimming, can only be learned by

getting in and striking out. It is impossible to learn to swim if your swimsuit never gets wet. We can give you all the instructions in the world, we can show you movies, we can tell you what it feels like, but there comes the time when you need to get wet! Once you are in the water we can begin to refine your style, but not before. As you come to the end of this book on evangelism can I urge you to 'get wet' evangelistically. There are many in the water calling out "It's great! Jump in!".

How many training courses have you done? How many books have you read? Has it resulted in you doing evangelism? Why don't you make it a matter of prayer? Start praying that God will cause you to love Him more. Pray that you will love people more and pray that God will give you boldness to do the work of evangelism. There is no doubt that God will answer that prayer, as He did on the two occasions it is prayed in the Bible. I have been greatly encouraged by these.

The first one is recorded in Acts chapter 4. Peter and John having healed the crippled man at the Gate Beautiful of the Temple were arrested because of their preaching. The Sanhedrin, which only a few months before had organised the death of Jesus, warned them to stop preaching the gospel. Peter's answer is wonderfully bold "Judge for yourselves whether it is right in God's sight to obey you rather than God. For we cannot help speaking about what we have seen and heard" (Acts 4:19,20). After further threats both Peter and John were released. When they rejoined their friends, there was much rejoicing and then prayer. That prayer is very revealing. It shows how really frightened they were, and with good cause! Their minds focused on the death of Jesus (Acts 4:25-28), and how this fulfilled God's promises about His Messiah (Psalm 2). No doubt the reference to Psalm 2 would have caused them to meditate on the fact that God promised the Messiah "to make the nations your inheritance" (Psalm 2:8), and to make Him a ruler who dashed His enemies "to pieces like pottery" (Psalm 2:9). So their prayer reaches a climax with these words "Now, Lord, consider their threats and enable your servants to speak your word with great boldness" (Acts 4:29). They wouldn't have prayed like that unless they were afraid. Was that prayer answered?

Luke tells us that "After they prayed, the place where they were meeting was shaken. And they were all filled with the Holy Spirit and spoke the word of God boldly" (Acts 4:31). It was a great answer.

Paul expresses himself in almost the same way. He was in prison awaiting trial. He wrote to the Ephesians and specially requested them to "Pray also for me, that whenever I open my mouth, words may be given me so that I will fearlessly make known the mystery of the gospel, for which I am an ambassador in chains. Pray that I may declare it fearlessly, as I should" (Ephesians 6:19,20). He was obviously apprehensive, so he asked his friends to pray that he would speak boldly. Was their prayer answered?

Paul describes it for us, "At my first defence, no-one came to my support, but everyone deserted me. May it not be held against them. But the Lord stood at my side and gave me strength, so that through me the message might be fully proclaimed and all the Gentiles might hear it..." (2 Timothy 4:16,17). A great answer!

Can I challenge you to pray for boldness and make it a priority? Ask your friends to pray for you also.

Joy—a powerful motive

Jesus tells us in the Parable of the Lost Sheep that "there is more rejoicing in heaven over one sinner who repents than over ninety-nine righteous persons who do not need to repent" (Luke 15:7).

There are no greater moments in the life of a Christian than the joy of experiencing his friends turning to Christ. I remember after preaching a sermon a man came to me and said, "I was thinking during that sermon that if I was killed today I would be in no fit state to face my Maker. Can you please tell me how I can pass from death to Life?" I could, and he did!!

My prayer is that you will know that joy again and again.

APPENDIX

Preaching Evangelistic Sermons

Some of you who read this book will be in teaching positions, or in Sunday Schools and youth clubs, lay preachers or as the minister of a congregation. As such you will be in a position from time to time to give evangelistic talks and sermons. This chapter is designed to help us clarify the principles which govern such talks.

Timothy is encouraged by Paul to "do the work of an evangelist, discharge all the duties of your ministry" (2 Timothy 4:1-5). It comes in an interesting context. Paul has been reminding Timothy of his obligations as a teacher and preacher. Part of that obligation is to do the work of an evangelist. All teachers of the Bible, by definition, must be able to teach those parts of the Bible which are evangelistic, the evangel. We must not drive a wedge between teaching and evangelism. The Bible doesn't. Paul reminded the Colossians that they *heard*, *understood* and *learned* the gospel from Epaphras (Colossians 1:6,7). Their evangelist taught them the gospel.

Evangelistic sermons are, generally speaking, like any other sermon. Their distinctive features are:—

Content of the sermon

The evangelistic sermon can be either a declaration of the gospel or an apologetic whereby the reasonableness of Christianity is explained. If the latter is used it should focus on the implication of the apologetic, namely the gospel, before it ends.

1. Stick to the text. I have already shown that the

gospel should focus upon Jesus (Romans 1:3) and so should the evangelistic sermon. It should aim to show who Jesus *is* and what He came *to do*. Why not keep a book in which you can note, from your daily Bible reading, passages which will be ideal to preach evangelistically, so that when the time comes you will have a good store available from which to draw. I often scribble down a few subheadings as a sermon outline to go with them like this:—

Mark 1:14,15	1. Jesus preaches God's gospel
	2. The gospel is about the kingdom
	3. Repent and believe the gospel
John 3:36	1. All are in one of two groups
	2. Believing on Jesus—Eternal Life
	3. Disobeying Jesus—God's wrath
Acts 17:30,31	1. Certainty of judgment—God's time fixed
	2. Agent of the judgment—Jesus risen
	3. God's requirement for judgment—repentance
Romans 10:9,10	1. Confess—Jesus is Lord
	2. Believe—God raised Jesus
	3. Certainty of salvation—you *shall*
Colossians 2:13-15	1. God cancels our debts
	2. God nailed them to the cross
	3. Jesus is Lord through the cross
Hebrews 2:14,15	1. Jesus shared our humanity
	2. Jesus' death destroyed death
	3. Jesus' death delivers from fear

2. Fresh and varied. A method like this will help to ensure that our evangelistic preaching will remain fresh and varied. It will save us from lapsing almost unconsciously into well used passages like John 1:11,12 and John 3:16 when we aren't really preaching on them. A variety of evangelistic sermons will be much appreciated by the congregation as well as the preacher. Like a diamond, the gospel has many facets which flash to us from the pages of the Bible.

Preachers who do expository preaching through books of the Bible know that they are frequently called upon to preach evangelistically. The text before them requires it. I came across a very good example of this in D. Martyn Lloyd-Jones' book *God's Ultimate Purpose* (Banner of Truth). This is a book of thirty-seven sermons preached from Ephesians 1:1-23. The three sermons on Ephesians 1:7 are strongly evangelistic. It would be difficult to preach faithfully on this verse and be otherwise!

The Bible abounds in good clear statements of the gospel in summary form and these should be used, but beware—the Bible is not an allegory, and remember— *stick to the text.*

I once heard an evangelistic sermon which began by declaring Jesus to be the One who was able to "raise" men and women from the death of sin to a new life of righteousness. "He is able" we were told, "to give a new beginning". Three parts of the Bible were used to show this. The raising to life of Jairus' daughter (Mark 5:35-43), the raising to life of the widow's son of Nain (Luke 7:11-15) and finally the raising of Lazarus from the dead (John 11:38-44).

Briefly the sermon went like this: "Firstly, age and sex are no barrier to being raised from the death of sin. Jesus is able to do so. He raised a small child, a young man and an old man. He can do it to you. Secondly, when Jesus raised Jairus' daughter He instructed that she should be given something to eat. When a person is made new by Jesus he should immediately take in spiritual food—to strengthen him. The Bible is the spiritual food and should be read to strengthen us in the spiritual life. Thirdly, the widow's son at Nain was given back to his mother, into a social setting. This shows that people who have been raised from the death of sin to the new life should not isolate themselves from other Christians but meet with them and fellowship with them. Fourthly, when Jesus called Lazarus back from the dead, He gave immediate instruction to untie him because his feet and hands were tied up with the linen grave clothes. This signifies that the new Christian is to have nothing to do with the things which belong to 'death'. There is to be a clean break from everything sinful". The sermon concluded with a strong appeal to all who were 'dead' to call upon Jesus to bring them to new life. The logical problem of the 'dead' speaking was not covered but it did occur to me as strange.

Everything in that *outline* is both true and biblical, but none of the *statements* is a true exposition of its text. The sermon is not in fact about Mark 5:35-43, Luke 7:11-15 or John 11:38-44. It is a sermon on Ephesians 2:4,5—"But because of his great love for us, God, who is rich in mercy, made us alive with Christ even when we were dead in transgressions—it is by grace you have been saved". The question which kept nagging at me was, "Why didn't he preach on Ephesians 2:4,5?" What he wished to say is clearly stated there.

Some people have defended this type of preaching on the basis that the content is true and biblical. There are two reasons why it is undesirable. First, those who listen to this preaching will approach the Bible as if it is an allegory and needs to be decoded. They will be looking for the message behind the message, and not the plain meaning of the words. By this method God's Word becomes something other than what the Bible says. Second, and of more importance is the fact that the true message of that part of the Bible is completely neglected. We were not directed to focus our minds on Jesus the Lord of life and death. We were not urged to trust Him who is 'resurrection and life'. I was not encouraged to put my faith in the One who can take me securely through death to resurrection. It is these truths the Gospel writers are stating in these passages, and so if I choose to preach on those texts, I should be true to the Bible and say clearly what it is clearly saying, because that is what God is saying.

I have often heard the story of the healing of Naaman's leprosy (2 Kings Chapter 5) used evangelistically. It would be a great surprise to me if the writer of 2 Kings ever thought that Naaman's healing really meant that we could have our sins forgiven through the death of Jesus! It would even surprise me if the writer of 2 Kings *knew* about the death of Jesus until the day he (the writer), died (but thankfully he knows now!). There are so many good clear statements of the gospel that there is no need for us to resort to creating allegories. Be fresh and varied in your approach, but stick to the text and find one which says exactly what the gospel is.

3. *Stick to the context.* Like all good expository preaching, the evangelistic sermon should make a clear statement of what the Bible is saying, and the selected passage should be expounded *within its context* whether that is the immediate chapter or the whole book.

John 1:12,13 is a classic statement of the gospel "Yet to all who received him, (Jesus) to those who believed in his name, he gave the right to become children of God— children born not of natural descent, nor of human decision or a husband's will, but born of God". There is a clear contrast made between the Jews who rejected Jesus (verse 11), and those who "received him and believed in his name". Everything hinges on the meaning of 'receiving Jesus'. What does it mean?

On every occasion I've heard this verse used, I have been told that I receive Jesus by asking him into my heart to cleanse me from sin. However, I doubt if John the Gospel writer, had that in mind in this passage. To receive Jesus in this context is to do the opposite to that which the Jews did. They rejected Him as 'the Word' who was in the beginning, who was with God and was God, who created all things and who is light and life (John 1:1-5). Consequently, for someone to have eternal· life he must receive Jesus *in the way* John has already described Him.

Another example of a verse used evangelistically outside its context is Revelation 3:20 "Here I am! I stand at the door and knock. If any one hears my voice and opens the door, I will go in and eat with him, and he with me." This verse is used universally to describe how we are to respond to Jesus. He is outside our life and wishes to come in. He knocks at the heart's door. He will not force His way in. However, if I personally 'open the door' of my life, Jesus will come into my life and change me.

I am not arguing against the truth of these statements, but I don't think John, the writer of Revelation, had that in mind in the passage. To start with, the passage is directed to the church members at Laodicea and not to individual unbelievers. I don't doubt that there were un-converted members in that congregation but it is not addressed to them specifically. It is addressed to *all* members. The church had lapsed into 'lukewarmness' (Revelation 3:16). Believing themselves rich they did not perceive either their true condition or their peril (Revelation 3:17,18). Jesus describes them as 'those whom I love'—they are obviously His already and so He 'rebukes and disciplines' them. They are called to repent because He is standing at the door (of the church?). He wishes them to return to true fellowship with Himself and to throw off the lukewarmness. What a wonderful passage to preach upon to rouse a church from complacency! Sadly, we never hear it in that capacity, it is always being directed to unbelievers.

Not only is it used in that way, but most sermons I hear are not really sermons on the text but a description of Holman Hunt's painting 'The Light of the World'. I have been told again and again about that door which has no handle on the outside, and that Jesus will not force His way in unless I let Him. Indeed, I am told, He *cannot* (not withstanding Paul's treatment on the Damascus Road (Acts 9) or Lydia's conversion (Acts 16:14)). I am presented with the perfect picture of the impotent Christ so ineffectual, that even a small child can hold the living God at bay! I am told that Christ longs to come into my life but cannot unless *I* open the door.

No one could arrive at that idea from Revelation 3. An unbeliever cannot open the door because he is 'dead' and needs new life (Ephesians 2:1), the verse is directed to believers and unbelievers.

The Jesus who stands at the door knocking is described as "...the Alpha and the Omega...who is, and who was, and who is to come, the Almighty" (Revelation 1:8). Standing in the midst of the churches, (symbolised in Revelation by seven golden candlesticks) with great dignity, power and majesty. His eyes are like blazing fire, and His voice like the booming of the surf on the shore. From His mouth proceeds the two-edged sword and His appearance such, that the writer fell before Him as though dead (Revelation 1:13-17). He is anything but impotent. He is the one who stands outside the church at Laodicea commanding repentance (Revelation 3:19) so there might be restored fellowship with Him.

There are so many clear statements of the gospel in the Bible that we do not need to resort to doubtful exegesis, but there is no doubt that the person who "stands at the door" is described in Revelation 1:7-18. This description must be born in mind when expounding Revelation 3:20.

I attended a conference for lay preachers and Bible study leaders. We were asked to come with a talk prepared on certain set passages of the Bible. We delivered these during the course of the conference. One of the passages selected was 1 Peter 3:18 "For Christ died for (your) sins once for all, the righteous for the unrighteous, to bring you to God". It is a wonderful part of the Bible. All the talks which were given were clear statements of the atonement. When we had heard them all, the person directing the weekend asked if we would be able to use exactly the same talk and just change the verse to 2 Corinthians 5:21, "God made him who had no sin to be sin for us, so that in him we might become the righteousness of God", or to 1 Corinthians 15:3,4, "For what I received I passed on to you as of first importance: that Christ died for our sins according to the Scriptures, that he was buried, that he was raised on the third day according to the Scriptures". Most of us agreed that we could use the same talk with minor changes. That probably meant that we hadn't really understood what God was saying to us in each of those passages. We didn't understand why the death of Jesus was spoken about within the context on each occasion. Did each writer use it for the same reason? I don't think any of us had ever thought about it.

Keep it simple

Clear statements are always *appreciated* in sermons but they are *essential* in evangelistic preaching. Technical terms should be used sparingly and always explained. The sermon should be well illustrated. Make an effort to keep the ideas down to two or three major ones. State the first idea, explain it, illustrate it and apply it before moving on to the next. It is important to remember the sermon is directed to unbelievers who, unlike the church members, may not be used to listening to sermons. They should be considered when the length of the sermon is planned. If Bibles are not available in the pews, have the passage printed on a handout with an outline of the sermon and even a prayer of commitment which people can pray at the end.

If the church Bibles are used, a brief statement explaining the chapter and verse numbering can be helpful. Several years ago I was doing some 'follow-up' with a young man who had just been converted. I gave him a Bible study comprehension to do which asked questions and gave a Bible reference where the answer could be found. We arranged to meet again, for me to check his completed comprehension. To my disappointment he had not answered any questions correctly.

When I asked him if he had looked up the verses, he said, "What verses?" I pointed out the verses at the end of each question. "I wondered what that meant but I couldn't work out who John was and I hadn't a clue what the figures 3:16 meant." I told him to forget the whole exercise. I explained the chapter and verse system, showed him the Bible's index and gave him the Bible study to do again. He arrived a week later with it completed—and correct.

1. Where is it heading? The evangelistic sermon is to be so directed that a person will respond positively to

Jesus in repentance and faith. It should move logically to that end and those terms should be carefully explained. For several years I attended a church where the minister regularly preached sermons which were strongly evangelistic but which never quite told us how we should take action. We knew we should do something but were never quite sure what.

When I have finished preparing an evangelistic sermon I ask myself the question, "Will a person who wants to respond to Jesus as a result of this sermon know *what* to do to turn to Christ?" This part needs to be well prepared and not just tacked on to the end. All evangelistic sermons must challenge people to act.

2. *To appeal or not?* When I preach evangelistically I usually conclude with a prayer incorporating both repentance and faith. I invite people to pray it with me, and provide them with an easy way by which they can show that they have repented and wish to turn to Christ. Sometimes I ask them to come out to the front of the church or to the Communion rails while we sing a hymn. Sometimes they are asked to wait in their seats as the others go. Sometimes I ask them to tell me or the minister after the service. Since I am always a visitor at someone else's church, I work out with the minister and the elders what will be the most satisfactory way to do this.

There are two reasons why I ask people to demonstrate their response.

First, it says to everyone "He means me to *do* something *now*". No one can be left in doubt that some action is required. They are required to make a choice. Some have objected that the choice may be 'to stay behind or not to' and which is quite different from accepting or rejecting the gospel. Care needs to be taken to make clear why such a demonstration is being called for.

It is essential to understand in evangelistic preaching, as in every area of evangelism, that faithfulness in preaching the gospel is what is important and *not* outward response (see Matthew 11:20). Response is a work of God. Many preachers are frightened to make a direct appeal in case no one responds and some have expressed the idea that if that is the case, and there is no response, it could not have been 'of God'. If it is right to do it, it will be so no matter what the response. Whether people respond immediately or not, it impresses upon them that we are taking the gospel seriously, response to it is urgent, and action is called for now. When a method like this is used, the congregation must be taught to judge the usefulness of evangelistic preaching not by the *outward response*, but by the *faithfulness of the preaching*. It will be helpful to discuss and teach this before the day of the event, rather than later.

Second, it is helpful to the new Christian. At the end of the sermon I explain "If you pray this prayer I'm going to ask you to stay in your place when the others leave. There are three reasons why I think this will help you. Firstly, you will have *done* something outwardly which says to all of us 'I've turned to Christ in repentance and faith'. Secondly, the other Christians will see you and will be able to start praying for you in a new way. Thirdly, I will be able to talk to you briefly about where you can get help in living the Christian life and give you some literature."

I must stress again how important it is to prepare 'the challenge to action' part of the sermon. On those occasions when I have not done so, inevitably I begin preaching a new sermon called 'the appeal'. It is often long and very muddled because I am excited as well as under attack from the devil not to do it. Prepare that section carefully and make sure that you plan enough time and the place in the sermon in which to present the challenge, so that the whole exercise does not become long and drawn out.

Many have had unfortunate experiences where long appeals have been tacked on to evangelistic sermons to exert psychological pressure on people to respond outwardly. We have all been subjected to singing that last chorus again for what seemed to be the umpteenth time and still seeing no one come out.

I once attended an evangelistic meeting where at the end of the sermon we were all asked to stand. Then the Christians were asked to sit down. Who was left standing?! Then all those who wanted to become Christians were told to sit. Who was left standing then?!!

The preacher then 'sermonised' until everyone standing wilted under the pressure. It was a disgraceful night where people were treated like things. We all object to that type of pressure.

Some people have shared with me their concern that if we tell people what to say in prayer, they may just repeat it even though no genuine work of regeneration of the Holy Spirit has taken place. Having done that they may falsely believe that they have become Christians and thus present us with a serious pastoral problem. I have much sympathy with this point of view and believe that when we call for outward response it must be with love, care and restraint, and that the people who respond should be counselled by responsible mature Christians. Done with care, the advantages are significant; it is not however, an essential feature of evangelistic preaching and should *never* be used as a substitute for real content.

Whether or not the preacher calls on people to make some overt response there should be no doubt in our preaching that God "commands all people everywhere to repent" (Acts 17:30).

The age of preaching has not passed. Evangelistic preaching should be the feature of every church. If it is not a part of your church's worship, start praying that a change will come. If you are the minister you may find it helpful to read 2 Timothy 4:1-5.

John Chapman

A FRESH START

A Fresh Start tackles some of life's fundamental questions, and points the way to an adventurous and exciting new life. In his clear, straightforward style, John Chapman provides a thorough investigation of Christianity. Part one examines what God has done through Jesus Christ; part two is for those who are uncertain about the existence of God and whether Jesus was his Son; part three shows the importance of responding to God and part four explains how to become a Christian and grow in faith.